Chef EATS

RECIPES AND TECHNIQUES

Alison MacNeil CCC
featuring Chef John MacNeil

One Printers Way
Altona, MB R0G 0B0
Canada

www.friesenpress.com

ISBN
978-1-03-914375-3 (Hardcover)
978-1-03-914374-6 (Paperback)
978-1-03-914376-0 (eBook)

1. COOKING, ENTERTAINING

Distributed to the trade by The Ingram Book Company

To my amazing husband John, thank you for sharing your knowledge and expertise, motivating, and always believing in me. Special thanks to my incredible mother for inspiring me to create this cookbook, editing my work, and seeing this project through to its delicious end!

Table of Contents

Introduction

I started cooking and working in professional kitchens when I was 14 years old. Fast forward 25 years and I can't imagine doing anything else.

My first job in a professional kitchen was at our local pizza joint in Strathmore, the town where I grew up, east of Calgary. Making fresh dough daily, slicing tender ham and spicy pepperoni, shredding cheddar, and mozzarella cheese . . . these were just the beginning of my passion for preparing delicious food.

I was in high school at the time and unsure of what I wanted to do after graduation when my food and nutrition teacher encouraged me to apply to SAIT's culinary program. That was the start of my formal education as a chef, and I'll never regret following my teacher's advice. I graduated with my journeyman certificate and went on to work in some of Calgary's finest restaurants.

My passion for the world's cuisines motivated me to travel abroad as much as possible, gaining the knowledge and experience I would need to take the next step of completing my Red Seal trade certificate and becoming a chef.

During the pandemic, I decided to take my career one step further, applied to the Canadian Culinary Institute, and graduated as Certified Chef de Cuisine. I never dreamed that my passion for preparing food would take me to where I am today. What I love most about being a chef is creating experiences and memories for my guests, then having them tell me, "That was the best meal I've ever had!"

I have learned so much in my career and have been exposed to many different cooking styles, cultures, and cuisines. The places I have worked and the countries I've visited, such as Spain, Italy, and France, have influenced my personal style and continue to inspire each recipe that I create.

In preparing to write this book, I sifted through my old notebooks. Many of the recipes I've written over the years look like shopping lists of ingredients with no measurements or method of preparation. I can remember scribbling down the ingredients before making the dish, thinking I'd fill in the details later.

These treasured notes are the basis for *Chef Eats*. In it, I'll explain some valuable techniques and share recipes for some of my favourite dishes. I've tested each recipe to arrive at the exact measurements, with easy-to-follow instructions.

In this cookbook, I am featuring recipes created in collaboration with my husband Chef John MacNeil. John and I have opened and worked together in several restaurants in Calgary.

We met at Teatro, an Italian fine-dining restaurant where I was hired as a line cook. I learned a lot about the art of cooking there. John, who was sous chef at the time, later took over as executive chef for the company. This was when he hired me as chef de cuisine to open Teatro's sister restaurant Cucina, an Italian-inspired bistro and market with made-to-order sandwiches, pastas, in-house-made charcuterie, and daily chef-inspired rotisserie dishes.

Our complimentary cooking styles have made us unique as a team. John specializes in fine dining with touches of molecular gastronomy, and my specialties are home-style cooking and comfort food. Much of my inspiration comes from Spain, having spent a lot of time with our Spanish family, shopping the colourful food markets, foraging for mushrooms in the Pyrenees mountains, and cooking together with them at their home in Vic, a small town outside of Barcelona.

I love the Spanish culture and cuisine, including the meticulously hand-cut *jamón*, creamy béchamel-filled croquettes, and beautiful tapas with all their flavours and textures. Dining in Spain is a truly extraordinary experience and I wanted to bring some of those flavours home to Canada.

Those travels spurred a milestone in my career: collaborating as co-chef with John at opening Black Pig, a Spanish-influenced bistro in Calgary's influential Bridgeland community.

The layout of my cookbook is based on the four stations I have worked in a professional kitchen. My goal was to master each station and, in doing so, work my way up to Chef.

The stations are as follows:

Garde manger, the preparation of appetizers and cold foods. This is typically a meal's first course, which sets the tone for dishes to come.

Next, I moved on and learned to prepare fresh pastas and pan items, such as creamy mushroom risotto or rabbit meatball pappardelle. This was my favourite station, turning out perfectly seasoned and creative dishes.

Next, I'd work on the meat and fish station, which was generally considered to be the most critical: timing is everything on a busy line. Meats and main dishes were to be ready to serve hot and, in some cases, meats rested to the perfect doneness just in time to send to the table.

Last was the pastry station, dishes to be served at the end of the meal, which could include a cheese course followed by dessert.

Some of the recipes I've included are simple, but it's important to note that the quality of the ingredients can make the greatest impact on the resulting dish. Using fresh ingredients when they are in season and shopping the local markets is the best advice I can give. All my recipes and techniques are adaptable and can be recreated with ingredients that are in season and available to you. Have fun cooking, try new things, and always take the recipe as a guideline, not a rule.

Happy cooking!

Specialty Equipment and Ingredients

I want to highlight a few specialty tools and ingredients to help you navigate *Chef Eats*.
Where possible, I will offer alternatives.

Salt	This is a common ingredient but one of the most important in some instances. I use Mediterranean Sea salt in almost all my cooking because I prefer that it is milder in flavour, enhancing product taste without an overpowering saltiness. Salt comes in many different colours, flavours, and textures, so try a few and decide which one you like best. There are no rules when it comes to salt, it's all about personal preference.
Pepper mill	Having a pepper mill is essential; freshly cracked black pepper is second to none. It's aromatic and spicy, with citrus, wood, and floral notes, most of which are lost in pre-ground pepper as it oxidizes quite quickly once cracked.
Mortar and pestle	Like black pepper, freshly ground spices are fragrant and full of flavour when compared to pre-ground spices. A mortar and pestle can also be used to crush garlic or grind nuts into a paste.
Scale	I prefer to measure ingredients in many recipes by weight to be more precise. Not all onions or peppers are the same size, weighing these items ensures the same outcome every time. Having a scale is important for a few of the recipes in *Chef Eats*. An example: for the cured items, weighing the salt, nitricure (see page 25), and the meats themselves can be crucial to the outcome.
Agar	This gelling agent is derived from red algae that has been dried and powdered; it's a vegetarian replacement for gelatin. Typically used in pastries and desserts, agar is also a common ingredient in molecular gastronomy.
Xanthan gum	Xanthan gum is a food additive that is used as a thickening agent and stabilizer to prevent the separation of ingredients. A little goes a long way with xanthan gum.

Citric acid	This organic compound found naturally in citrus fruits is used as a preservative and flavouring agent.
Malic acid	Malic acid is an organic compound found naturally in apples and pears. Malic acid contributes to the sour taste in fruits and can be used as a food additive and flavour enhancer.
Nitricure 1 & 2	Sodium nitrite is used for curing meats, blocking the growth of bacteria, and preventing spoilage. Nitricure #1 is used for curing meats that will require cooking afterwards, such as bacon, smoked ham, or sausages. Nitricure #2 is used for curing meat products that will be air-dried instead of cooked or smoked, like dry-cured salami, air-dried beef, or *coppa*.
Butchers twine	Butchers twine is an oven-safe string used to truss chickens or tie a roast holding it in a uniform shape during cooking.
Carta fata	Carta fata is a transparent cooking film that allows you to cook up to 440°F without the use of oil or fat if desired. The package holds in all the juices and flavours from the food being cooked inside.
Parchment Paper	Heat, grease, and moisture resistant, parchment paper is used for lining baking trays to prevent sticking; it can also be used to cook *en papillote*. It is compostable or there are many types of reusable tray liners that work as well.
Blender	A blender is ideal for items that have a lot of liquid, like smoothies and soups. I love to use my blender for turning out velvety smooth fruit and vegetable purées, sauces, and even blended cocktails.
Food processor	This is a convenient tool for chopping, grating, or mixing ingredients faster than if you do it by hand. I use my food processor for emulsifying salad dressings and dips or grating parmesan cheese into a fine powder.
Stand mixer	A stand mixer is great for making cookies, cakes, doughs, breads, or anything whipped. There are many different attachments for a stand mixer making it easy for you to grind your own meat, roll out fresh pasta dough, or make your own ice cream.
Pasta sheeter	This machine is essential for creating fresh pasta at home. A manual countertop sheeter is inexpensive and easy to use. If you make a lot of fresh pasta at home and have a stand mixer, it might be worth investing in the pasta sheeter attachment.
Vacuum sealer	If you are someone who likes to shop in bulk, then a vacuum sealer is the perfect tool to have. Packing ingredients in an airtight environment can help prolong their shelf life significantly, especially when freezing meats, fish, fruits, or vegetables.

Grill	Using a grill or a BBQ is a way to add charred flavour and aroma to meats and vegetables. I also use my BBQ to smoke meats, a package of wood chips over the grill works just as well if you don't have a smoker.
Deep fryer	A deep fryer is a kitchen appliance used to cook food completely submerged in oil at a high temperature, generally 350°F–375°F. A basket is used to lower the food into the oil. You may also use a deep pot on the stove for deep frying. Make sure to use a thermometer to hold the temperature, where specified, while frying.
Thermometer	I prefer to have a thermometer that has a high-temperature range. This way it may be used to check the temperature of hot oil when deep frying on the stovetop. Also, use your thermometer to check the internal temperature for the doneness of a steak or roast.
iSi canister	An iSi canister is a food whipper used for the easy creation of fresh whipped cream, aerated batters, and foams. A nitrous oxide (N_2O) cartridge is added to the pressurized canister mixing with the liquid of choice and turning out amazingly light, aerated products.
Squeeze bottle	You will need a squeeze bottle to make the pomegranate pearls on page 47. They are also useful for storing and extruding oils or any variety of salad dressings or sauces.
Tamis	This kitchen utensil is shaped like a drum with a fine mesh screen and used as a strainer, grater, or food mill. For the gnocchi recipe on page 77, pressing the potatoes through a *tamis* will turn out softer textured gnocchi. Alternatively, a fine mesh strainer will work.
Fine mesh strainer	Also known as a *chinois*, a fine mesh strainer is like a tamis but is bowl-shaped with a finer screen. It can be used for straining sauces, stocks, or purées, sifting flour, rinsing rice, or washing vegetables.
Slotted spoon	This kitchen utensil has holes for easy draining or removing products from a liquid.
Canning jar lifter	Use this tool to remove hot jars from boiling water. They fit around the jar and are coated in rubber to make them non-slip.
Canning rack	This wire rack fits in the bottom of a large pot and keeps the jars elevated and away from the heat of the stovetop element.
Mason jar	These glass jars with bands and lids that seal are used for canning and preserving a variety of foods. The jars can be reused but the seal should only be used once.
Cooling rack	This kitchen tool is used to hold hot products straight from the oven, allowing for even cooling.

Ring cutters	I use these the most for cutting pastry or pasta rounds ready for a variety of fillings. They also work for cutting cookies or biscuits.
Mandolin	This slicer has a wide platform to easily guide fruits or vegetables over a sharp fixed blade. A mandolin can be used to create fruit or vegetable chips, julienned carrots, or thinly sliced cabbage for coleslaw.
Pastry bag (piping bag)	Used commonly for pastries, cake decorating, and icing, a pastry bag is a cone-shaped bag made of paper, plastic, or cloth. The bag is fitted with a nozzle, or piping tip, to create different shapes and decorations.
Pastry brush	This kitchen utensil is useful for brushing egg wash on pasta dough to seal stuffed pastas or over pies to create a golden crust.
5-inch pie plates	In this cookbook, I use these foil tin pie plates to make individual **Chicken Pot Pies** (page 95). You may also want to make a full 9-inch chicken pot pie. Cut it into pieces, then serve.
4-inch fluted tart shells	Fluted tart shells are typically used to make a variety of small, sweet, or savoury tarts. In this book, I will use them to create individually sized pies in the **Faux Apple Pie** recipe on (page 121).
Ramekin	A ramekin is a small heat-resistant baking dish. I use them in this book for the **Pumpkin Sticky Toffee Pudding** recipe (page 131) to create small-sized cakes. Alternatively, the recipe works using a square brownie pan.

Glossary of Culinary Terms

Antipasto refers to the first course of a meal, traditionally in Italian cuisine. Antipasto consists of an assortment of ingredients such as cured meats, cheese, olives, pickles, and marinated vegetables.

Basting involves pouring the melted fat or cooking juices over the food to keep it moist.

Batonnet is a rectangular, stick-shaped knife cut measuring a 1/2 inch by 1/2 inch by 3 inches.

Beef bung is the appendix of a cow preserved in salt and used in the production of large, cured meats and sausages.

Beurre blanc is a warm butter sauce. Cold butter is emulsified into a reduction of vinegar or wine and shallot.

Blanching is the process of scalding food, typically vegetables or fruit, in boiling water for a short time, then into an ice bath to immediately stop the cooking process.

A boning knife has a long, thin, and flexible blade for easy boning of meats, poultry, or fish. It has a sharp tip and blade making it easy to remove connective tissue and separate meat from the bone.

Braising is a combination cooking method using both wet and dry heat. The food is generally seared or grilled at high heat first, submerged in a liquid, and covered to simmer or stew slowly in an oven.

Broccolini is a hybrid of broccoli and Chinese broccoli, or *gai lan*. Broccolini has small florets at the top of long slender stalks.

Brunoise is a fine dice culinary knife cut. Typically, a fruit or vegetable is first julienned, then turned and diced finely.

Caramelization is the browning of a food's natural sugars, giving it a nutty sweet flavour and dark brown colour.

A channel knife   is a sharp carving tool used commonly for cutting citrus zest that can be mixed into various cocktails.

Charcuterie   is a French term referring to the art of creating prepared and cured meats such as salamis, pâtés, rillettes, sausages, and bacon. In addition, the term may refer to a deli-style shop in which these meats are sold.

Chimichurri   is a sauce or marinade common in Argentinian cuisine. It's typically served as a condiment alongside grilled meats, and is made with chopped parsley, garlic, olive oil, and chili pepper.

A cleaver   is a large blade knife typically used for chopping through animal bone.

Deglaze   refers to adding a liquid to a hot pan to remove the browned bits of seared or sautéed food that adds flavour to the final product.

A Dutch oven   is a large heavy cooking pot with a tight-fitting lid, commonly made from cast iron, but can also be cast aluminum or ceramic.

Dredge   means to lightly coat a portion of food in a dry ingredient, such as flour, for the purpose of deep-frying the food crispy.

En papillote   is French for "enveloped in paper," a cooking method where the food is wrapped up like a parcel, typically with parchment paper, and baked.

Emulsify   means to combine two ingredients that normally wouldn't mix such as oil and vinegar.

Garde manger   refers to the station in a professional kitchen, typically an entry-level position for cooks.

Glace de viande   is a gelatinous reduction of stock used as a flavouring agent in recipes or as a sauce on its own.

Infusion   is the process of soaking an ingredient in a liquid such as water, alcohol, oil, or vinegar to extract its flavour.

An iSi canister   is used for the easy creation of fresh whipped cream, aerated batters, soups, and foams. A nitrous oxide (N_2O) cartridge is added to the pressurized canister, mixing with the liquid of choice, and turning out amazingly aerated products.

Julienne   is the method of cutting an ingredient into thin strips that resemble fine matchsticks.

Manchego   is a semi-firm Spanish cheese made from the milk of Manchega sheep from the La Mancha region in Spain and aged from 60 days up to two years. The cheese has a slightly crumbly texture with a rich nutty flavour.

Mirin   is a type of fermented rice wine used commonly in Japanese cuisine.

Molecular gastronomy	scientifically views food, nutrition, and culinary processes through chemistry and physics.
A muddler	is a bartending tool used to smash different ingredients to a flavourful pulp, which will be mixed into a drink or cocktail.
Non-reactive	refers to the type of metal a container is made from. Glass, stainless steel, and ceramic are non-reactive, while cast-iron, aluminum, and copper are reactive.
A paring knife	has a small blade, making it versatile in the professional kitchen; it is used for jobs that require precision cutting or peeling.
Roux	refers to a mix of flour and fat cooked together and used to thicken sauces or soups.
Sabayon	is the technique of turning egg yolks, sugar, and a liquid, typically sweet wine, into a light fluffy custard served on top of fresh fruit.
A saucepot	is a deep pot typically used for boiling large amounts of liquid or stewing.
A saucepan	is smaller and shallower compared to a saucepot, with higher sides than a frying pan. It's typically used for making quick sauces or something that requires stirring and constant attention like risotto.
Sauté	is a cooking method using a frying pan on high heat with a little oil or fat.
Scoville Heat Units	refers to the amount of capsaicin present in a chili pepper, the higher the number the hotter the pepper.
Sweat	refers to the cooking method of using a frying pan with a little oil or fat on medium heat and stirring frequently so that the ingredient becomes softened and translucent, not browned.
Temper	is the method of melting chocolate to a specific temperature, then cooling and heating again producing a shiny surface and snap in texture to the final chocolate.
Tourné (turned)	is a classical French knife cut. Typically, vegetables like potato or squash are cut into a barrel shape consisting of seven sides.
Trussing	refers to tying a large cut of meat or roast with butchers' twine to retain its shape and hold in juices while cooking and resting.
A turning knife	has a sharp, curved blade used for peeling or creating turned vegetables or fruits.
Umami	is the fifth taste receptor commonly found in meat broths, fermented foods, and other ingredients including aged cheese, tomatoes, and mushrooms.
Macerated	refers to the process of soaking food in a liquid to soften it, typically raw fruits, or vegetables.

Fresh food markets in Vic, Barcelona, and Blanes, Spain

Garde Manger

Garde manger refers to the station in a professional kitchen, typically an entry-level position for cooks. I spent a lot of time in my career working as a garde manger cook, perfecting a variety of cold dishes and small plates, including charcuterie items such as pates, terrines, cured meats, or pickles. A few of the restaurants I worked in required the garde manger cook to also make pastries or the garnishes for dessert and cheese plates.

Salted Butter

Hot Sauce

Pickled Mustard Seeds

Pickled Fennel

Maple Bacon

Coppa

Bresaola

Spiced Marcona Almonds

Olive Trio

Sobrassada Croquettes

Green Gazpacho

Tomato Caesar Salad

Grilled Peach Salad with Pomegranate Pearls

Steak Tartare

Salted Butter

Homemade butter is easy to make and provides more essential fatty acids than commercially produced butter. In this recipe I use 52 percent cream from grass-fed cows, sourced from a local organic dairy farm. Cows grazing on grass store beta-carotene in their fat, which is released when the cream is churned. The churned butter that results will be vibrant yellow in colour and a delicious, more vitamin-rich option.

The buttermilk that is separated from the butter can be used in recipes such as biscuits or fried chicken.

Yield: Approximately ½ lb
Recipe time: 10 minutes + overnight

2 cups **52% heavy cream**
½ tsp **salt**

Specialty equipment
Stand mixer

FOR THE BUTTER

Pour the cream into the bowl of a stand mixer fitted with the whisk attachment.

Turn the speed on high and whip the cream until it separates, 5–10 minutes, then turn the mixer off.

Place a fine mesh strainer over a mixing bowl. Pour the separated cream into the strainer.

Wrap the bowl, leaving the butter inside the strainer to allow it to drain. Refrigerate overnight.

The next day, remove the butter from the fridge and let it warm to room temperature.

Place the butter into a mixing bowl and fold in the salt.

Press the butter into a silicone mould or form it by hand.

Keep your butter in the refrigerator in a sealed, airtight container.

CHEF NOTES

Allowing the buttermilk to drain completely will result in longer shelf life for the butter.

Hot Sauce

The sky is the limit on the many variations you'll find for hot sauce! They can be mild, medium, hot, or scorching. They might be cooked and puréed or fermented and aged for desired flavour. But hot sauces all contain one common ingredient: some variety of chili pepper.

A jalapeño pepper has 2,500 to 8,000 Scoville Heat Units, which makes them mild in comparison to serrano, habanero, or ghost peppers, which have over one million Scoville Heat Units. All peppers start green. As they are left on the plant to mature, they change colour, resulting in a hotter pepper with sweeter flesh than the unmatured fruit. For this recipe, I have used red jalapeños to try to capture a level of heat and sweetness for a balance of flavour in the sauce.

Yield: 4 cups
Preparation time: 2 hours + 24 hours
Cook time: 1 hour

1½ lb **pimento peppers**; seeded weight
5 oz **red jalapeño peppers**
2 oz **garlic**, peeled (8 cloves)
5 oz **white onion**, chopped

Specialty equipment
Blender
Fine mesh strainer

2 tbsp **salt**
2 cups **apple cider vinegar**
2 cups **water**
2 tsp raw **honey**

FOR THE HOT SAUCE

Wash the peppers thoroughly. The pimento peppers have many nooks and crannies for dirt to hide.

Quarter the pimento peppers and remove the seeds and the pith. Discard.

Cut off the stem end of the jalapeño peppers, then cut the peppers in half. Leave the seeds inside the jalapeño.

Mix the peppers, garlic, onion, and salt in a large mixing bowl. Wrap the bowl and leave it to sit on the counter at room temperature for 24 hours.

After 24 hours, pour the contents of the mixing bowl into a saucepot.

Add the apple cider vinegar and water.

Turn the pot on high heat and bring it to a boil, then turn the heat down to a low simmer.

Cook the peppers until they have softened, approximately 45 minutes.

Turn the heat off and pour the contents of the pot into a blender. Purée until smooth.

Set a fine mesh strainer over a bowl. Strain the hot sauce. Use a spatula to help press the liquid through the strainer.

Mix the raw honey into the sauce.

Allow the sauce to cool. Store it in a sealed container in the refrigerator. The hot sauce will keep for up to a month.

CHEF NOTES
For a milder sauce, remove the pith and seeds from the jalapeño peppers before salting them.

Notes

Pickled Mustard Seeds

Mustard is one of the condiments I use most. Whether it's prepared yellow mustard, grainy or Dijon, sweet, sour, or hot, I use it in many different recipes.

I'd like to show you two ways to prepare this delicious condiment, starting with pickled mustard seeds. They are great for adding a little crunch to a charcuterie or cheese plate.

Then, I'll make the pickled mustard seeds into spreadable mustard. Simply purée them in a blender after they have been pickled; the mustard may be used as a spread in your favourite sandwich or as an ingredient in salad dressing recipes.

Yield: 12-oz mason jar
Total time: 15 minutes + 1 week

Specialty equipment
Fine mesh strainer
Blender

¼ cup **yellow mustard seeds**
2 tbsp **brown mustard seeds**
2 tbsp **black mustard seeds**

1½ tsp **salt**
¼ cup **white sugar**
½ cup **white vinegar**

FOR THE MUSTARD SEEDS

Use a fine mesh strainer to wash the mustard seeds thoroughly with cold water. Allow to drain for 5 minutes and pour them into a mason jar.

In a small pot on high heat, bring the salt, sugar, and vinegar to a boil.

Turn the heat off and pour the liquid over the mustard seeds.

Allow the mustard seeds to cool completely. Store sealed in the refrigerator.

Let the seeds pickle for a week before using them.

To make the mustard spreadable, add the contents of the jar of pickled mustard seeds to a blender and purée.

Store the mustard sealed in the fridge.

CHEF NOTES

Try adding honey to the mustard when you purée it for sweeter style mustard.

Pickled Fennel

Fennel is at the top of my list of versatile fall ingredients, as it can be paired beautifully with many different flavours, savoury or sweet. There are two common varieties of fennel, one grown for its potent fennel pollen and dried fruit that's used as a spice. The other, Florence fennel, is treated as a vegetable. It has leafy greens that resemble dill and a large white to pale green bulb at the base of the plant. It can also be used as a fresh herb and the bulb has a mildly sweet anise or licorice-like flavour.

Fennel has a crunchy fibrous texture like celery, and it can be eaten raw, shaved thinly in a salad with olive oil and lemon juice. Its texture can withstand high temperatures in cooking, making it perfect for pickling, and it holds up well in braising, stewing, or grilling.

Yield: 4 x 16-oz mason jars
Preparation time: 2 hours
Cook time: 25 minutes

Specialty equipment
Mason jar
Canning rack
Canning jar lifter

2 lb **fennel bulbs, including stalks and fronds**
3 tbsp **salt**
2¼ cups **sugar**

2⅓ cups **water**
3 cups **white vinegar**

FOR THE PICKLED FENNEL

Wash the fennel. Cut the green stocks off the bulb and trim them to a size that will fit into jars for canning. Place them into a large bowl.

Quarter the fennel bulb, keeping the core intact to hold the layers together. Add the fennel to the bowl.

Mix the salt with the fennel and let it sit for 1 hour.

Place a wire canning rack on the bottom of a large pot. Fill with water and set it aside.

In a separate pot, bring water to a boil. Sterilize jars and seals by boiling them for 10 minutes. Remove the jars and seals from the water and place them on a clean tray.

Lightly squeeze the water from the fennel and add it to the sterilized jars.

Mix the vinegar, sugar, and water in a saucepot on high heat. Bring it to a boil, then pour the boiling liquid into each jar over the fennel. Fill the jars ¼ of an inch from the top.

Use a clean towel to dry the edges of the jars. Put the lids on each jar and add them to the large pot on the wire canning rack.

On high heat, bring the pot to a boil and boil the jars for 15 minutes.

Turn the heat off. Carefully remove the jars from the pot using a canning jar lifter. Let the jars cool to room temperature.

Tighten the lids, they may become loose when boiled, and check that they have all sealed. The pickled fennel will keep in a pantry or refrigerator for up to a year.

CHEF NOTES

The fennel can also be pickled in a non-reactive container with a tight-fitting lid.
Pour the hot pickling liquid over the fennel to cover and store in the refrigerator.

Notes

Maple Bacon

Curing is the process of preserving food by adding salt to remove moisture. Bacon is simple to make at home, it's delicious, and it doesn't contain the preservatives that are added to commercially produced bacon. Bacon is also versatile! Serve your bacon fried golden and crispy at breakfast or use it as an ingredient in savoury pasta dishes. Add bacon to a braised meat to infuse it with flavour or cover a roasted chicken with a layer of bacon to keep it moist and delicious.

Maple syrup, combined with aromatic herbs and spices creates the perfect sweet, salty, savoury bacon.

Yield: 2–3 lb bacon
Preparation time: 2½ hours
Curing time: 6 days

Specialty equipment
Scale
Cooling rack
BBQ or Smoker

2–3 lb **pork belly**

Maple Cure
2 tbsp **salt**
1 cup **brown sugar, loosely packed**
½ cup **maple syrup**
1 tsp **fresh thyme leaves**
1 tsp **juniper berries** (20 berries)
   lightly crushed

½ tsp **coriander seed**, toasted and cracked
1 tsp coarsely cracked **black pepper**
1 oz **garlic** (6 cloves), sliced

CURING THE PORK BELLY

Put the pork belly into a non-reactive container.

Mix all the ingredients for the maple cure in a bowl and pour it over the pork belly.

Wrap the container and store it in the fridge. Turn the belly over every other day for 5 days.

After 5 days, rinse the pork belly under cold water. Dry the belly with a paper towel and place it onto a cooling rack. Let the pork belly sit in the refrigerator overnight, uncovered to dry.

SMOKING THE BACON

Preheat a smoker or BBQ to 200°F.

If using a smoker: add a pan of applewood chips. Smoke the cured pork belly for 2 hours, adding more wood chips as needed.

If using a BBQ: wrap the wood chips in heavy-duty tin foil and poke a few small holes in it. Put the package over low flames on one side of the BBQ, wait for it to start smoking, and turn down the heat.

Cook the bacon in the BBQ on the opposite side of the wood chips for 2 hours. You may need two or three packages of wood chips.

Turn the heat off. Cool the bacon completely, wrap, and store it in the fridge. The bacon is now ready to be enjoyed on its own, sliced thin and fried crispy, or used in a variety of recipes.

CHEF NOTES

Use your maple bacon fried crispy in a BLT or crumbled on top of a classic Caesar salad.

Coppa

Coppa is a pork cold cut made from curing a pork shoulder's whole muscle group that runs from the neck to the fourth or fifth rib bone. For this recipe, I have used a piece from a whole bone-in pork shoulder. You can also ask your butcher to cut you a fresh coppa roast for curing if you prefer not to buy a whole shoulder.

Serve your coppa as an antipasto sliced thin, accompanied by other cured meats, pickles, olives, and cheeses.

Yield: 1 coppa
Preparation time: 2–3 hours
Curing time: 1½–4 months

Specialty equipment
Scale
Butchers' twine

3–4 lb piece of **pork shoulder or coppa roast**

Salt Cure
½ tsp **nitracure #2** (3 g)
⅓ cup **salt** (60 g)
¼ cup **brown sugar** (50 g)
2 tbsp **fresh cracked black pepper** (10 g)
1½ tbsp **orange zest** (9 g)
1 tbsp **coriander seed**, toasted and ground (5 g)

Casing and Dry Rub
1 fresh **lemon**
1 beef **bung**
2 tbsp **smoked paprika** (15 g)
2 tsp **dried chili flakes** (4 g)

FOR THE SALT CURE
Mix the ingredients in a bowl.

CUTTING THE PORK

Remove a ⅓ section of a whole pork shoulder, opposite the shoulder blade bone. Set the piece with the bone aside; it can be used for other recipes.

Trim the edges of the cut piece to make it more even all around. Record the weight of it.

CURING

Place the piece of shoulder in a non-reactive container. Rub it thoroughly with half of the dry cure mix.

Cover and refrigerate for 7 days, turning it over every 2 days.

On day 7, drain the liquid from the container. Rub the shoulder with the second half of the cure and refrigerate for another 7 days, turning every 2 days.

FOR CASING AND DRY RUB

Place the beef bung into a container. Cover it with cold water, cut the lemon in half, squeeze it slightly to release some of the juice and add it to the container. Soak the beef bung overnight in the lemon water the day before the shoulder is ready.

The next day, prepare the beef bung for stuffing by rinsing it thoroughly with cold water.

Remove the coppa from the container it was curing in. Rinse off the cure with cold water. Pat dry.

Mix the smoked paprika and chili flakes in a small bowl. Rub the outside of the coppa with a spice mix.

Stuff the coppa into the rinsed beef bung. Press out any air bubbles, making sure the coppa is completely wrapped.

Tie the coppa like a roast, using butchers' twine spaced evenly around the coppa.

Hang the coppa in the refrigerator to dry. This process takes up to 3 months; the coppa is ready when it has lost 30 to 40 percent of its original weight.

Because you are curing inside the refrigerator, use a spray bottle filled with fresh water and lightly spray the coppa every day. This will keep the beef bung from drying out before the coppa is ready. Alternatively, you may use a drying chamber set between 50°F to 60°F and 60 to 70 percent humidity.

The finished coppa should feel firm; squeeze it to check. If it is still soft to the touch, continue curing it.

CHEF NOTES

Check out the cider-braised pork shoulder recipe on page 101 to see how to use the rest of the pork shoulder.

Bresaola

is typically made using beef eye of round, which is salted then air-dried for one to three months. During this curing period, the meat will become firm and dark red in colour. Traditionally, bresaola is sliced paper-thin, drizzled with olive oil and lemon juice, and served with fresh arugula or parmesan cheese. You can also use your bresaola in sandwiches or as charcuterie alongside salami and other cured meats.

Yield: 1 cured eye of round
Preparation time: 1–1½ hours
Curing time: 1–3 months

3–4½ lb **beef eye of round**

Salt Cure
1 tbsp **juniper berries** (40 berries)
¼ cup **fresh rosemary leaves** (6 g)
2 tbsp **fresh thyme leaves** (4 g)
⅔ cup **salt** (100 g)
⅓ cup **brown sugar** (70 g)
1 tbsp **fresh cracked black peppe**r (6 g)
2 tsp **dry mustard powder** (4 g)
½ tsp **garlic powder** (2 g)

Specialty equipment
Scale
Butchers' twine

FOR THE SALT CURE

Finely chop the juniper berries, rosemary, and thyme leaves.

Combine with the rest of the ingredients in a mixing bowl. Set it aside while you prepare the beef.

TRIMMING THE BEEF

Using a sharp boning knife, cut the fat and sinew off the beef. Record the weight after it has been trimmed.

CURING

Put the beef into a non-reactive container. Rub the outside of it with half of the dry cure mix. Cover it and refrigerate for 7 days. Turn the beef over every 2 days.

On day 7, drain the liquid out of the container and wash it out.

Rub the beef with the other half of the dry cure and place it into the washed container for 5 more days. Turn the beef again every other day.

After the second week, rinse the beef with cold water. Pat it dry and tie it with butchers' twine, like you would a roast, evenly spacing the ties. Hang it in the fridge to dry; this will take up to 3 months.

When curing meats inside the refrigerator, it is important to make sure the outside of the meat doesn't dry out before the inside is ready. Allow the bresaola to dry for a few days then fill a spray bottle with fresh water and lightly spray the outside of the beef every day.

The bresaola is ready when it has lost approximately 40 percent of its original weight.

CHEF NOTES

In Calgary our climate is dry. Adjust the curing instructions based on the humidity of your climate.

Notes

Spiced Marcona Almonds

These lightly spiced almonds are cooked low and slow in oil to create the perfect crunchy salty snack. Serve them with your favourite beverage at a dinner party or make up a big bowl to enjoy while watching the game.

Marcona almonds are often called the queen of almonds. They are imported from Spain and almost exclusively grown there. Marcona almonds are rounder and are known for their mildly sweet flavour and creamy texture, comparable to the macadamia nut. For this recipe, I've added paprika for its smokiness and tomato powder to balance the sweetness of the almond.

Yield: **2 cups**
Preparation time: **15 minutes**
Cook time: **45 minutes**

2 cups **Marcona almonds**

1 cup **canola oil**

1½ tsp **sweet smoked paprika**

½ tsp **tomato powder**

1 tsp **salt**

1 tsp **oil from cooking the almonds**

FOR THE ALMONDS

Put the almonds into a small saucepot and cover them with the canola oil.

Cook the almonds on low heat until they start to turn golden brown, about 45 minutes. Stir occasionally for even browning.

Place a fine mesh strainer over a bowl.

Turn the heat off and carefully strain the almonds from the oil.

Place the almonds, smoked paprika, tomato powder, salt, and 1 teaspoon of the oil from cooking the almonds into a mixing bowl. Toss together until the almonds are coated evenly.

CHEF NOTES

Try adding hot smoked paprika to give the almonds a spicy kick.

*O*live Trio

I love olives! Making an olive dish rekindles memories of shopping in the markets of Spain, with their fresh produce piled high and arranged in every colour of the rainbow. My favourite displays were the olives, always temptingly organized by shades of earth tones, reds, greens, and blacks. Some were marinated with herbs and spices, submerged in a fiery red pepper sauce, stuffed with roasted garlic, or simply brined. Olives are versatile and delicious. For this recipe, I will prepare three separate olive dishes, highlighting a few of my favourite ways to eat these delicious briny fruits.

Kalamata Olive Tapenade

Yield: **1 cup**
Preparation time: **30 minutes**

Specialty equipment
Food processor

6 oz **pitted kalamata olives**
1 clove **garlic**
1 tbsp **brined capers**

¼ cup **extra virgin olive oil**
1 tbsp **fresh parsley leaves**
2 tsp **fresh oregano leaves**

FOR THE TAPENADE

Remove the kalamata olives from the brine and pat them dry on a paper towel. Do the same with the capers.

Place all the ingredients into a food processor and purée. Remove the tapenade from the food processor and serve or store in an air-tight container in the fridge for up to two weeks.

CHEF NOTES

Olives will add salt to any recipe as they undergo curing and fermentation, which adds brininess to the fruit. I haven't added salt to this recipe, but taste and season the tapenade as desired.

Garlic Pepper Manzanilla Olives

Yield: 1½ cups
Preparation time: 45 minutes + overnight
Cook time: 10 minutes

Specialty equipment
Blender

10 oz **red bell pepper** (2 peppers)
3 tsp **garlic** (4 cloves)
3 tbsp **olive oil**
¾ tbsp **cumin seeds**, toasted and ground
½ tsp **crushed red pepper flakes**

½ tsp **paprika**
¼ tsp **salt**
¼ tsp **red wine vinegar**
7 oz **manzanilla olives**

FOR THE OLIVES

Cut the bell peppers in half and remove the pith and seeds. Chop the peppers into a small dice.

Mix all ingredients, except the olives, in a saucepot and sauté on medium heat. Continuously stir the mix to sweat the vegetables without browning them.

Once the peppers are soft, approximately 10 minutes, turn off the heat.

Pour the mixture into a blender and purée until smooth.

Remove the olives from the brine or oil they are packed in and pat them dry. Place the olives into a container with a tight-fitting lid, pour the purée over top, and mix. Allow the olives to cool, then cover them and marinate overnight in the fridge.

CHEF NOTES

Manzanilla olives are small green olives, the most common variety of olive in Spain.

Stuffed Queen Olives

Yield: Approximately 50 pieces
Preparation time: 1–1½ hour

Specialty equipment
Pastry bag and small, round piping tip

10 oz **queen olives**
1 oz **piparra peppers** (7–10 peppers)
3½ oz **chèvre cheese**

¼ tsp **honey**
Pinch of **salt**

FOR THE STUFFED OLIVES

Remove the piparra peppers from the brine and pat them dry.

Chop the piparra peppers and place them into a mixing bowl. Mix them with chèvre, honey, and salt.

Put the cheese mixture into a pastry bag fitted with a small, round piping tip. If you don't have piping tips, simply cut a small piece off the end of the pastry bag.

Pipe the cheese mixture into each olive.

Place olives on a serving dish. Drizzle with olive oil and garnish with sliced piparra peppers.

CHEF NOTES

Piparra peppers are small, long green peppers from the Basque region in Spain.

Sobrassada Croquettes

When I think of Spanish food, tapas immediately come to mind. Of the many different tapas and bar snacks, croquettes are my go-to favourites when I am hosting a dinner or casual get-together. Filled with rich creamy fillings, breaded, then deep-fried to golden perfection, these tasty snacks are a definite crowd-pleaser.

Typically, Spanish croquettes are made with *jamón*, but for this recipe, I have used sobrassada, which gives the croquettes a little more spice and pairs well with rich Manchego béchamel. Sobrassada is a raw, cured sausage made from ground pork, seasoned with paprika, and salt, originating in the Balearic Islands. It has a soft and spreadable texture, lightly rendered to remove some of its fat, which is used to cook the béchamel sauce.

Yield: **28–30 1-oz pieces**
Preparation time: **2½ hours + overnight**
Cook time: **30 minutes**

Specialty equipment
Deep fryer

Croquette Filling
3½ oz **sobrassada**
3 cups **whole milk**
¼ cup **salted butter**
1 tsp f**at from sobrassada**
⅔ cup **all-purpose flour**
1 tsp **salt**
2 oz **Manchego cheese, grated**

Croquette Breading
3 cups **panko breadcrumbs**
4 **eggs**, beaten
½ cup **flour**

FOR THE FILLING

Peel the casing off the sobrassada and cut it into fine pieces.

Place the sobrassada into a small frying pan on medium heat. Cook just until the fat starts to render. This will take about 2 minutes and it should resemble oily ground meat.

Drain through a strainer placed over a mixing bowl to catch the rendered fat. Set the meat aside.

Pour the milk into a saucepot on medium heat. Bring the milk to a boil and turn off the heat. Stir occasionally to prevent the milk from scalding.

Put the butter and sobrassada fat into a saucepot on high heat.

Once the butter has melted, add the flour, whisking continuously to make a roux. Cook the roux for about 2 minutes.

Turn the heat down to medium and start adding the hot milk one cup at a time. Whisk in-between additions, making sure the mix is smooth.

Once all the milk has been added, turn the heat to low. Simmer the sauce for 15 minutes. Stir occasionally to prevent it from burning.

Turn the heat off. Mix in the sobrassada meat, Manchego cheese, and salt.

Pour the filling onto a small baking tray lined with plastic wrap. Spread it out to about 1-inch thickness. Cool completely in the refrigerator, wrap the tray and let it set overnight.

FOR THE BREADING

Preheat a deep fryer to 350°F.

Set up three shallow containers, one with all-purpose flour, one with beaten egg, and one with the panko breadcrumbs.

Cut the croquettes into approximately 1-ounce pieces. If the mix is quite soft, place the tray into the freezer for 5–10 minutes to make it a bit easier to work with, but do not freeze.

Drop the pieces into the flour first. Coat the croquettes evenly then place them into the egg and then the panko crumbs, coating them evenly.

Gently reshape the croquettes to form a cylindrical shape.

Dip the croquettes back into the egg. Finally, roll them into the panko, making sure they are evenly coated.

Carefully add the croquettes to the deep fryer. Fry the croquettes until they are golden brown, about 3 minutes.

Remove from the fryer onto a paper towel to catch any excess oil.

Season the croquettes with a sprinkle of salt and serve.

CHEF NOTES

You may also want to try making croquettes with dry-cured chorizo, jamón ibérico, or a mix of parmesan and Manchego cheeses for a crispy cheesy snack.

Notes

_____

_____

_____

_____

_____

_____

_____

_____

_____

_____

_____

_____

_____

_____

_____

_____

_____

_____

_____

_____

_____

_____

_____

Green Gazpacho

Gazpacho is a soup that originated in the southern region of the Iberian Peninsula between Spain and Portugal. Gazpacho is made with raw, blended vegetables, fresh herbs, and spices, and is served cold, which is refreshing on a hot summer day. To create my green version of this classic dish, I have used tomatillos as an alternative to red tomatoes and added Santa Claus melon, fresh fennel, cilantro, and lime juice.

Yield: 4 cups
Preparation time: 45 minutes

1½ cups **tomatillos**, quartered
14 oz **santa claus melon**, peeled, seeded, and diced
1 cup **cucumber**, peeled and seeded
1 cup **yellow bell pepper**, seeded and chopped
1 cup **fennel bulb**, chopped
¼ cup **fresh cilantro leaves**
¼ cup **olive oil**

Specialty equipment
Blender

2 cloves **garlic**
2½ tbsp **fresh lime juice**
2 tsp **honey**
1 tsp **salt**

Finishing the Plate
Lime zest
Cucumber, sliced thin
Cilantro

FOR THE GAZPACHO

Add all the ingredients to a blender.

Purée the gazpacho until it is smooth.

FINISHING THE PLATE

Pour the gazpacho into bowls and garnish it with lime zest, cucumber slices, and fresh cilantro.

CHEF NOTES

Also known as Christmas Melon or Piel de Sapo, Santa Claus melon has a pleasantly sweet, pale green-to-white flesh with a thick, green-striped rind.

Tomato Caesar Salad

There's something invigorating about picking a shiny, colourful tomato right off the vine. The smell of the velvety soft leaves and the perfect ripeness of the fruit itself have led me to create my tasty tomato salad.

This dish is inspired by both the Canadian Caesar cocktail and the classic Caesar salad. These influences, along with the best-quality tomatoes make this salad stand out. Vine-ripened tomatoes and aged cheese, like Grana Padano, have a high concentration of umami flavour and combine well in a salad to create a deliciously savoury dish you will enjoy and remember.

Yield: Serves 4
Preparation time: 2 hours

Tomatoes
1½ lb **cherry tomatoes**

Parmesan Dressing
1 **egg yolk**
3 tsp **Dijon mustard**
3 tbsp **lemon juice**
3 oz **Grana Padano cheese,** grated
1 large clove **garlic,** chopped
1 tsp **capers,** chopped
1 tsp **salt**
1 tsp **fresh cracked black pepper**
1¼ cups **canola oil**

Specialty equipment
Food processor
Slotted spoon

Brown Butter Crunch
½ cup **panko breadcrumbs**
1 tbsp **butter**
¼ tsp **salt**

Fried Capers
½ cup **canola oil**
¼ cup **brined capers**

Finishing the Plate
Olive oil
Salt
Grana Padano, shaved
Fresh basil leaves

FOR THE DRESSING

Place all the ingredients except oil into a food processor and blend.

Start adding the oil in a slow stream to emulsify the dressing.

Refrigerate the dressing in an airtight container while you prepare the rest of the salad.

FOR THE CHERRY TOMATOES

Trim the stem end from the tomatoes. Discard.

Place ice and water into a container or mixing bowl to make an ice bath.

Fill a saucepot with water and bring it to a boil on high heat.

Drop the tomatoes into the boiling water for about 30 seconds.

Turn off the heat, take the tomatoes out of the water using a slotted spoon, and put directly into the ice bath.

Remove the skins and allow the tomatoes to dry on a paper towel. Set aside.

FOR THE BROWN BUTTER CRUNCH

Preheat an oven to 350°F.

Place panko crumbs on a small baking tray and toast in the oven. Stir occasionally until they have turned golden brown, 8–10 minutes. Put in a mixing bowl and set aside.

In a saucepot, melt the butter on high heat. Stir the butter frequently until it starts to foam. The butter is ready when you can see the milk solids turning brown and the butter has a caramel aroma.

Turn the heat off and immediately pour the browned butter into the panko.

Add the salt and mix to combine. Set aside.

FOR THE CAPERS

Warm the canola oil in a small saucepan on medium-high heat.

Remove the capers from their brine and pat them dry.

Add the capers to the hot oil. Be careful; they may pop a bit.

Fry the capers for 1–2 minutes until they are golden brown and crispy.

Using a slotted spoon, remove the capers from the oil and onto a paper towel to drain.

FINISHING THE PLATE

Spread the dressing into the bottom of a bowl.

In a mixing bowl, gently toss the tomatoes with a touch of olive oil and a pinch of salt.

Arrange the tomatoes on the dressing.

Garnish the tomatoes with a sprinkle of brown butter breadcrumbs, fried capers, shaved Grana Padano cheese, and fresh basil leaves.

CHEF NOTES

Capers are the green, unripe flower buds of the caper bush and are typically salted or brined.

Grilled Peach Salad with Pomegranate Pearls

In this recipe, I transform pomegranate juice into pearls to simulate the sweet and sour seeds of the pomegranate fruit. To create the pearls, I use agar, which is a gelling agent derived from red algae that is dried and powdered. Agar is also used as a vegetarian-friendly substitute for gelatin in desserts and pastries and is commonly used in molecular gastronomy.

The ratio of juice to agar powder for the pearls works with any type of fruit juice. You might also try making pearls using balsamic or other types of vinegar. The mouth-watering sweet and tart fruits in this recipe match perfectly with salty jamón ibérico and Manchego cheese.

Jamón ibérico is a variety of jamón, a cured leg of pork derived from the black Iberian pig, commonly found in the central and southwestern region of the Iberian Peninsula, which includes both Spain and Portugal.

Yield: Serves 4
Preparation time: 2 hours

Specialty equipment
Fine mesh strainer
Slotted spoon
Squeeze bottle
Grill

Grilled Peach Salad

3 **peaches**
5 oz **Manchego cheese**
4 oz **jamón ibérico**
4 oz **arugula**

Olive oil
Salt

Pomegranate Pearls
⅔ cup **pomegranate juice**
1 tsp **agar powder** (3 g)

FOR THE PEARLS

Fill a metal container with canola oil about 2 inches deep. Place it into the refrigerator for at least 2 hours or overnight. The oil needs to be cold for the juice to set into pearls.

Prepare an ice bath that fits underneath the oil container, a slotted spoon, a fine mesh strainer, and a separate container with pomegranate juice to hold the finished pearls.

Add the pomegranate juice and agar powder to a small pot and turn it on high heat.

Whisk the mixture continuously and boil it for 1 minute at a hard boil. This will activate the agar powder.

Turn off the heat and carefully pour the juice into a squeeze bottle. Allow it to cool slightly before putting on the lid.

Slowly squeeze the pomegranate mixture into the cold oil. This will create a stream of droplets in the oil. They should sink and will set right away. If some are floating, gently mix the oil so they sink. Do this in batches so the oil remains as cold as possible. If the pan has too many pearls at once they may fuse.

After about 2 minutes, use the slotted spoon and scoop out the pearls into a strainer to drain.

Once you've used all the juice, rinse the pearls under cold water and place them into the container of fresh pomegranate juice. Set them aside while you prepare the salad.

FOR THE SALAD

Preheat a grill on high heat.

Wash the peaches, cut them in half, remove the pit, and discard.

Drizzle the peaches with canola oil and grill them for about 5 minutes per side.

Arrange the peaches in the centre of a platter.

Mix arugula, olive oil, and salt in a mixing bowl and place on top of the peaches.

Garnish the salad with slices of jamón ibérico, shaved Manchego cheese, and pomegranate pearls.

CHEF NOTES

Try the salad with nectarines or pears as a substitute for peaches. You may even want to try this salad with beets in the winter months when stone fruits are not in season.

S teak Tartare

Tartare is a dish classically made using minced raw beef or horse meat, but the term has also been generalized to include other dishes made with raw meat or fish. Steak tartare is often made with chopped meat mixed with onions, capers, and seasonings, and served topped with a raw egg yolk. Turning the egg yolk into a sabayon gives this tartare a light, creamy texture, and the truffle, infused into the Manchego, gives the dish a subtle mushroom aroma. For this recipe, I have paired the tartare with salty potato chips, and a tangy parsley and shallot salad.

Yield: Serves 4
Preparation time: 30 minutes

Tartare

8 oz **beef tenderloin**

2 tbsp **pickled gherkins**

2 tbsp **brined capers**

2 tbsp Pickled Mustard Seeds
(recipe on page 17)

1 tbsp **olive oil**

3 tsp **Dijon mustard**

1 oz **Truffle Manchego cheese**, diced small

1 tsp **salt**

Sabayon

2 **egg yolks**

1 tsp **red wine vinegar**

1 tsp **water**

½ tsp **sugar**

Finishing the Plate

1 bunch **Italian flat-leaf parsley leaves**

1 **shallot**, thinly sliced

1 tbsp **red wine vinegar**

Pinch of **salt**

Salted potato chips

FOR THE TARTARE

Remove the pickles and capers from their brine and chop finely. Add them to a mixing bowl and set aside.

Using a sharp boning knife, trim the fat and connective tissue off the tenderloin. Discard.

Chop the tenderloin fine. Add it to the mixing bowl with the capers and pickles and mix to combine with the rest of the ingredients.

FOR THE SABAYON

Fill a small pot with about 2 inches of water. Place on the stove and set on medium heat.

In a mixing bowl, combine the egg yolks, vinegar, water, and sugar.

Place the bowl over the pot of simmering water and whisk constantly until the mixture becomes light and fluffy. Remove the bowl every few seconds to allow some of the steam to escape and to keep the yolks from becoming overcooked.

FINISHING THE PLATE

In a small mixing bowl, combine the parsley leaves and shallot with the red wine vinegar and salt.

Divide the tenderloin mix over four plates.

Top the tartare with the sabayon and freshly cracked black pepper. Serve with the parsley salad and your favourite salted potato chips.

CHEF NOTES

Striploin or sirloin steak work as a substitute for the tenderloin.

Notes

Mercado de La Boqueria, a fresh food market in Barcelona

Pasta & Co.

The ultimate in comfort foods, fresh pasta is worth the effort to make at home. Fresh pasta dough is delicate and tender, cooks faster than dried, and can be mixed into a wide variety of sauces or filled with delectable ingredients.

In a restaurant kitchen, the pasta station typically includes other frying pan-cooked items such as risotto, gnocchi, sauces, or purées. I have included a few of my favourites in this chapter. The pasta dough recipe can be used to create any number of dishes you enjoy.

Pasta Dough
Smoked Ham Hock Tortellini
Rabbit Meatball Pappardelle
Bison Lasagna

Mushroom Broth
Mushroom Risotto
Baked Potato Gnocchi

*P*asta Dough

I enjoy making pasta at home, spending a rainy afternoon inside making stuffed ravioli or tortellini, and experimenting with different fillings of braised meats or puréed vegetables. Have fun with it; there are no limits to what you can create with the perfect pasta dough.

This is the first pasta recipe that I learned when I worked as a young cook. I use a stand mixer and a vacuum sealer but making the dough by hand works just as well. If you're making pasta dough by hand, start by mixing the flour, salt, and olive oil; then turn it out onto a work surface and make a well in the centre. Place the eggs inside the well and start whisking them together until the dough forms a ball. Knead the dough until it has a smooth texture. Wrap it and allow it to rest in the fridge for at least 1 hour.

Yield: **2 lb pasta dough**
Preparation time:
15 minutes + 30 minutes resting time

3½ cups **all-purpose flour** (500 g)
2 tsp **extra virgin olive oil**
1 tsp **salt**

Specialty equipment
Stand mixer
Vacuum sealer

3 **whole eggs**
8–10 **egg yolks**

FOR THE PASTA DOUGH

Add the flour, salt, and olive oil to the bowl of a stand mixer with the paddle attachment.

Turn it on low speed and start adding the whole eggs one at a time.

Slowly add the egg yolks until the dough just comes together but is not sticky. Turn the mixer off.

Place the dough in a vacuum seal bag and seal the dough under full pressure. Allow it to rest for 30 minutes.

CHEF NOTES

When making a stuffed pasta, add an extra yolk or two for a softer dough which makes it easier to fill. For lasagna sheets or noodles, the dough can be firmer.

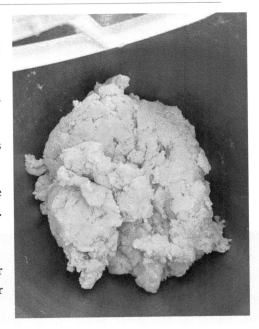

Smoked Ham Hock Tortellini

Harvest is my favourite time of the year. Summer has been spent tending and caring for each crop, then harvesting, cutting, and collecting your season's growth before the cold weather hits.

Parsnips are a root vegetable harvested in the fall. It is similar in shape to the carrot, with cream-coloured flesh that is slightly sweeter. They have an incredibly creamy texture when cooked and puréed.

I enjoy making stuffed pasta, and in this recipe, I have paired smoky ham with buttered peas, a classic flavour combination with the silky parsnip purée.

Yield: Serves 4
Preparation time: 6 hours + overnight
Cook time: 3 hours

Specialty equipment
Dutch oven
Blender
Pasta sheeter
Pastry brush

Braised Ham Hock
2 tbsp **canola oil**
1 cup **onion**, peeled and chopped
½ cup **carrot**, peeled and chopped
½ cup **celery**, chopped
½ cup **white wine**
1 **Roma tomato**
1 **smoked ham hock**
4 **cloves of garlic**
5 **fresh thyme sprigs**
2 **bay leaves**
1 tsp **black peppercorns**
8 cups Chicken Stock (recipe on page 91)

Filling
12 oz **ham hock meat** (1 ham hock)
1 tbsp **canola oil**
¼ cup **shallot**
1 tsp **Dijon mustard**
1 tbsp **parsley**, chopped
1 cup **braise reduction**
Salt
Fresh cracked black pepper

Tortellini Assembly
1 **egg**, beaten

Buttered Sugar Snap Peas
8 oz **sugar snap peas**
2 tbsp **butter**
Salt

Parsnip Purée
12 oz **parsnips**, peeled and chopped
1¾ cup **whole milk**
1 tsp **salt**
3 tbsp **butter**

FOR THE BRAISED HAM HOCK

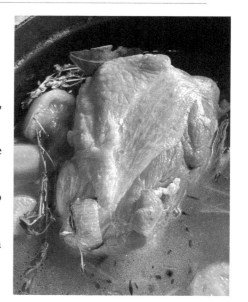

Preheat an oven to 285°F.

Heat the canola oil in a Dutch oven on high heat.

Add the onions, carrots, and celery to the pot. Cook, stirring frequently until the vegetables start to brown.

Deglaze the pot with white wine and cook until the wine has almost completely evaporated.

Add the rest of the ingredients and bring the liquid to a simmer.

Cover the pot with a tight-fitting lid, place it into the oven and cook for 3 hours.

Take the pot out of the oven and remove the lid.

Cool the ham hock in the braising liquid overnight in the refrigerator.

FOR THE FILLING

Remove the ham hock from the liquid and set it aside.

Strain the braising liquid through a fine mesh strainer into a saucepot. Turn it on medium heat. Simmer the liquid until it reduces to 1 cup. Cool and set aside.

Separate the ham hock meat from the bone and fat and discard.

Chop the meat into smaller pieces. Put it into a mixing bowl and set it aside.

Peel and brunoise the shallot.

Heat the canola oil in a small frying pan on high heat. Sweat the shallot until it softens and becomes translucent.

Turn the heat off. Cool the shallot and add it to the mixing bowl with the ham hock meat, chopped parsley, Dijon mustard, and reduced braising liquid.

Mix and season it to taste with salt and fresh cracked black pepper.

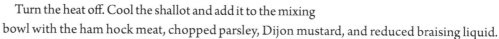

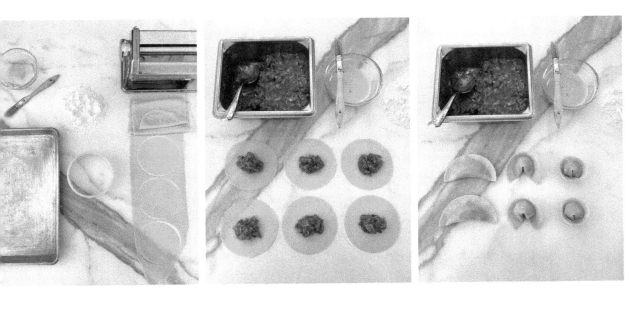

MAKING THE TORTELLINI

For the pasta, you will need about 14 ounces of pasta dough (page 57).

Cut the pasta dough into smaller pieces to make it easier to work with.

Lightly flour your work surface. Using a pasta sheeter, start rolling out the dough.

Start on the thickest setting, roll the dough through each setting until you have reached the thinnest setting.

Next, fold the pasta back into itself, and roll it through again. Repeat this step two more times.

Lightly flour the sheet of pasta and cut out rounds using a 4-inch cutter.

Drop tablespoonfuls of ham filling into the centre of each round.

Brush the edges of the pasta with the beaten egg.

Pinch the edges together in a half-moon shape.

Fold the corners together and pinch all the way around to make sure the pasta is sealed.

Place the tortellini on a tray dusted with flour.

The tortellini can now be cooked or frozen if you are making them ahead of time.

FOR THE PEAS

Fill a saucepot with water and season with salt, the water should taste a bit salty. Bring it to a boil on high heat. Add the sugar snap peas to the boiling water and blanch for 2 minutes.

Remove the peas from the pot and plunge into an ice bath to cool immediately and retain their bright green colour. Remove from the ice bath and set aside.

FOR THE PARSNIP PURÉE

Place the parsnips, salt, and milk in a small pot on medium heat. Cook until they are fork tender.

Add the parsnips to a blender with half of the milk and the butter. Purée until smooth. Add more milk if the mixture is too thick.

Pour the parsnip purée into a container and set it aside.

FINISHING THE PLATE

In a saucepot, add water and salt and bring it to a boil.

Add the tortellini and cook for about 8 minutes.

Add the butter to a large frying pan and melt on medium heat.

Remove the tortellini from the boiling water. Place into the frying pan with the melted butter.

Add the blanched peas to the pan and heat through.

In a small saucepot, add the parsnip purée and turn it on high heat. Stir frequently until it is hot.

Add a spoon of the parsnip purée to the centre of a plate. Top with the tortellini, and buttered peas then serve.

CHEF NOTES

Stuffed pasta is also a great way to use up leftovers. Try stuffing the tortellini with any chopped braised meats or roasted vegetables.

Rabbit Meatball Pappardelle

Pappardelle is a broad, flat, ribbon-shaped pasta noodle typically served with hearty meat or ragu-type sauces. Making pappardelle is as simple as rolling out sheets of pasta then cutting them into wide strips.

For this recipe, rabbit meatballs are braised in tomatoes, fine herbs, and spices, simple and delicious, highlighting the flavour of the rabbit meat. Rabbit is an excellent source of lean, protein-rich meat, commonly prepared braised or stewed. The taste of rabbit is often compared to chicken, but I find it has a gamier more intense flavour that pairs well with the fresh pappardelle noodles, stewed tomatoes, thyme, and garlic.

Yield: Serves 4
Preparation time: 2 hours
Cook time: 1 hour

Tomato Sauce
3 tbsp **olive oil**
½ cup **shallot**, diced small
1 oz **garlic**, sliced thin (6 cloves)
1 cup **white wine**
3½ lb **Roma tomatoes**, chopped
1 tbsp **fresh thyme leaves**
1½ tsp **salt**
1 tsp **sugar**
½ tsp **paprika**

Specialty equipment
Pasta sheeter
Scale

Rabbit Meatballs
1 tbsp **olive oil**
1 **shallot**, minced
2 **cloves of garlic**, minced
1 lb **ground rabbit**
¼ cup **panko breadcrumbs**
1 **whole egg**
2 tsp **salt**
¼ tsp **fresh cracked black pepper**
Fresh thyme leaves
Grated parmesan cheese

FOR THE TOMATO SAUCE

Pour the olive oil into a saucepot on medium heat.

Add the shallots and garlic and sweat for about 3 minutes.

Deglaze the pot with the white wine and cook until the wine has almost completely evaporated.

Add the rest of the ingredients and turn the heat down to a low simmer.

Cook the sauce for 30 minutes, stirring occasionally to prevent it from burning.

FOR THE RABBIT MEATBALLS

In a small frying pan, heat the olive oil on high heat.

Add the shallot and garlic and sauté until soft, about 2 minutes. Turn the heat off and remove the shallots and garlic from the pan.

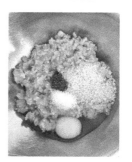

Cool the mix and combine it with the rest of the ingredients in a mixing bowl. Mix well. Weigh out 20-gram portions of meat and roll into balls.

Heat a large frying pan with 1 tablespoon of oil on high heat. Add the meatballs and brown them on all sides.

Reduce the heat to low, add the tomato sauce, and cook for 20 minutes. Stir the meatballs occasionally.

ROLLING THE PASTA

For the pasta, you will need about 14 ounces of pasta dough (page 57).

Cut the pasta dough into smaller pieces, making it easier to work with.

Lightly flour your work surface. Using a pasta sheeter, start rolling out the dough. Start on the thickest setting, roll the dough through each setting until you reach the thinnest setting.

Next, fold the pasta back into itself, roll it through again, and repeat the rolling process one more time.

Lightly flour the pasta, fold it loosely, and cut into ¼-inch strips.

FINISHING THE PLATE

Fill a saucepot with salted water and turn it on high heat.

Add the pasta noodles to the boiling water and mix. Cook the noodles for 2 minutes, strain, and add them to the rabbit meatball pan.

Mix the meatballs and pasta and turn off the heat.

Divide the pasta and meatballs into bowls. Garnish with fresh thyme leaves and grated parmesan cheese.

CHEF NOTES

You can also try using ground chicken, pork, or veal for this recipe.

Bison Lasagna

Mouth-watering layers of fresh pasta, braised bison, creamy caramelized onion béchamel, and loaded with mozzarella and Grana Padano cheese, this lasagna is decadent and delicious.

Perfect to serve for a large family or gathering of friends, this dish can also be made ahead of time, cooked, portioned, and frozen to be enjoyed individually.

For this recipe, I have used bison meat, which is leaner than beef and is an excellent source of complete protein; it's also rich in essential vitamins and minerals. I like the meaty flavour that bison adds to this lasagna after it has been slowly braised in sweet San Marzano tomatoes and red wine.

Yield: Serves 6
Preparation time: 3–4 hours
Cook time: 2–3 hours

Bison Sauce

2 tbsp **olive oil**
½ cup **yellow onion**, diced small
¼ cup **celery**, diced small
¼ cup **carrot**, diced small
1 tbsp **garlic**, minced (3 cloves)
1 lb **ground bison**
1 cup **red wine**
28-oz **can of whole San Marzano tomatoes**
3 tbsp **tomato paste**
2 tsp **salt**
1½ tsp **sugar**
1 tsp **fresh thyme leaves**, chopped
1 tsp **fresh rosemary leaves**, chopped
1 tsp **dried oregano**
¼ tsp **Worcestershire sauce**

Specialty equipment

Pasta sheeter

Caramelized Onion Béchamel

2 tbsp **canola oil**
3 cups **yellow onion**, diced
¼ cup **butter**
¼ cup **all-purpose flour**
2 cups **whole milk**
1 tsp **salt**
½ cup **Ricotta Cheese** (recipe on page 113)

Lasagna

Bison meat sauce
Pasta sheets
12 oz **mozzarella cheese, grated**
3½ oz **Grana Padano cheese, grated**
Caramelized onion béchamel
Fresh basil leaves
Fresh cracked black pepper

FOR THE BISON SAUCE

Heat 1 tablespoon of the oil in a saucepot on medium heat.

Add the onions and cook until they start to brown, stirring frequently.

Next, add the carrot, celery, and garlic to the saucepot.

Sauté the vegetables until they start to soften. Remove the vegetables from the pan and set aside.

Place 1 tablespoon of oil in the pot. Add the bison and cook, stirring often until the meat is browned.

Add the vegetables back into the pot and stir. Then add the red wine and cook until the wine has almost completely evaporated.

Add the rest of the ingredients to the pot and turn the heat to low.

Simmer the sauce for 45 minutes. Remove the sauce from the pan into a container to cool.

FOR THE BÉCHAMEL

Pour the canola oil into a saucepot and turn it on medium heat.

Add the onions and cook, stirring occasionally, until they become golden brown and caramelized. This will take about 45 minutes.

Remove the onions from the pot and let cool completely. Set aside.

Heat the milk in a separate saucepot on medium heat.

In another saucepot on high heat, melt the butter. Add the flour to create a roux and cook for 2 minutes, whisking continuously.

When the roux resembles white sand, turn the heat down. Start pouring in the hot milk about a half cup at a time. Whisk in between each addition until the sauce has a smooth consistency.

Turn the sauce to low heat and cook for 15 minutes, stirring occasionally to prevent it from burning.

Turn the heat off the sauce and pour it into a container to cool completely.

In a mixing bowl, combine the caramelized onions, béchamel, and ricotta cheese. Set aside.

ROLLING THE PASTA

You will need approximately 14 ounces of pasta dough (page 57).

Using a pasta sheeter, start rolling out the dough. Start on the thickest setting, roll the dough through each setting until you reach the thinnest setting.

Next, fold the pasta back into itself, roll it through again, and repeat the rolling process one more time.

Cut the pasta into sheets to fit inside a lasagna pan or 9-inch by 13-inch cake pan.

Fill a pot with water and salt and bring it to a boil on high heat. Add the pasta sheets and cook for 2 minutes.

Remove the pasta from the water into an ice bath to cool. Layer the sheets in between plastic wrap or parchment paper to prevent them from sticking together.

FOR THE LASAGNA

Preheat oven to 350°F.

First, add a thin layer of the bison sauce to the pan, then start layering the lasagna.

Add a sheet of pasta, then a layer of bison sauce with a light sprinkle of mozzarella and Grana Padano cheeses.

Then add another sheet of pasta, a layer of caramelized onion béchamel, and a light sprinkle of cheeses.

Continue with one more layer of each sauce and end with a pasta sheet, a thin layer of bison sauce and the rest of the cheeses.

Cover the lasagna with foil and bake it in the oven for 45 minutes. Make sure the foil creates a dome over the lasagna, so the cheese doesn't stick to it.

For the last 15 minutes remove the foil and cook the lasagna until it is golden brown.

Remove the lasagna from the oven and cut it into portions.

Plate the lasagna and garnish it with fresh basil and freshly cracked black pepper.

CHEF NOTES
Use the recipe for Ricotta Cheese (page 113) or store-bought works great too.

Mushroom Broth

I use shiitake mushrooms as a base for this recipe. I like them for their meaty, umami flavour, perfect for infusing into this broth. Native to East Asia, shiitake mushrooms can be easily cultivated under the right conditions and are readily available.

This recipe is versatile and can be used as a vegetarian stock replacement for soups, side dishes, or even vegetable braises. Save the mushrooms for making the broth. They can be chopped, mixed with sautéed garlic, shallots, cream, and fresh parsley then used as a filling for fresh pasta.

Yield: 6 cups
Preparation time: 45 minutes
Cook time: 2 hours

2 tbsp **canola oil**
1 **yellow onion**, julienned
4 **cloves garlic**, chopped
½ cup **white wine**
1 lb **fresh shiitake mushrooms**
    or (3½ oz **dried shiitake**)
1 **Roma tomato**

Specialty equipment
8-quart stockpot
Fine mesh strainer

1 **bunch parsley, stems only**
2 **celery sticks**
3 **sprigs of fresh thyme**
1 tsp **salt**
1 tsp **whole black peppercorns**
12 cups **water**

FOR THE BROTH

In an 8-quart stockpot, heat the canola oil on medium heat. Add the onion and sauté, stirring occasionally until it starts to brown. Add the garlic to the pot and cook for 1 minute.

Deglaze the pot with the white wine and cook until the wine has almost completely evaporated.

Add the rest of the ingredients, turn the heat to low, and simmer the broth for two hours.

Turn the heat off. Strain the broth through a fine mesh strainer. Store the broth in an airtight container in the refrigerator for up to a week or freeze for later use.

CHEF NOTES

I use this recipe for the Mushroom Risotto (page 73).

Mushroom Risotto

Risotto is one of my favourite dishes to cook. It is rice that is slowly simmered in broth or stock, absorbing flavours added to it until it reaches a rich and velvety consistency.

For this recipe, I have combined morel and porcini mushrooms and paired them with a rich shiitake broth. Garnishing the dish with black trumpets, combined with the other mushrooms and Grana Padano cheese, creates an umami savouriness on the palate.

Three types of Italian rice can be used to make risotto: arborio, carnaroli, and vialone nano. My go-to is carnaroli, which creates a creamy risotto that, when finished with mascarpone cheese, becomes a wonderfully decadent dish.

Yield: **Serves 4**
Preparation time: **2 hours + overnight**
Cook time: 1 hour

Mushroom Risotto
½ oz **dried morel mushrooms**
½ oz **dried porcini mushrooms**
½ oz **dried black trumpet mushrooms**
½ **yellow onion**, small diced
½ cup + 2 tbsp **butter**
¼ cup **canola oil**
1¼ cup **carnaroli rice**
1 tsp **salt**
½ cup **white wine**
4–6 cups Mushroom Broth (page 71)
½ cup **mascarpone cheese**
2 oz **Grana Padano cheese**
Salt
Fresh cracked black pepper

Finishing the Plate
Rehydrated black trumpet mushrooms
2 tbsp **butter**
2 cloves **garlic**, sliced thin
½ cup **Italian parsley leaves**
Mushroom Broth (page 61)

FOR THE RISOTTO

Put the dried mushrooms (morel, porcini, and black trumpet) into separate containers and cover with cold water to rehydrate them. Put them into the fridge overnight.

Pour the mushroom broth into a saucepot on medium heat.

Add 2 tablespoons of butter and 1 tablespoon of canola oil to a high-sided saucepan and turn it on high heat.

Squeeze excess water from the mushrooms and reserve the black trumpets for garnish later.

Add the porcini and morel mushrooms to the pan and sauté. Cook for about 3 minutes, stirring until they start to brown. Remove the mushrooms from the pan and set aside.

Add a ½ cup of butter to the pan with 2 tablespoons of canola oil.

Add the diced onion and salt. Cook until the onion is soft and translucent.

Stir in the rice and toast for about 2 minutes, stirring constantly.

Deglaze with white wine and cook until the wine has completely evaporated.

Turn the heat to low and start adding the mushroom broth 1 cup at a time.

Stir the rice once after adding the broth and let it be absorbed before adding another cup and stirring again.

After 3 additions of broth, add the sautéed mushrooms into the risotto and continue adding broth until the rice is tender. Reserve a few tablespoons of broth for plating.

Turn off the heat. Add the cheeses and stir until they are melted and incorporated. Add salt and pepper to taste.

FINISHING THE PLATE

Squeeze the excess water from the black trumpet mushrooms.

In a frying pan on high heat, melt the butter and add the mushrooms and garlic. Cook for about 2 minutes, stirring occasionally.

Stir in the parsley and turn the heat off.

Divide the mushroom risotto into 4 bowls.

Top the risotto with the black trumpet mushrooms.

Spoon a small amount of the mushroom broth around the outside of the risotto and serve.

CHEF NOTES

I use dried mushrooms for the risotto, but fresh ones can also be used, especially when they are in season.

Notes

Baked Potato Gnocchi

For this recipe, I have recreated the simple flavours of a baked potato in a plate of gnocchi. The gnocchi in this dish are pillowy soft and covered with rich chicken *glace de viande*, garnished with crispy potato skins, sour cream, and green onion.

Gnocchi is a dumpling made from potatoes and several different ingredients, which may include flour, semolina flour, cheese, vegetables, or herbs. Originating in Italy, the recipes for gnocchi vary across the different regions. Enjoy them as a dish on their own or as a side dish with a grilled steak, roasted chicken, or vegetables.

Yield: Serves 4–6
Preparation time: 2–3 hours
Cook time: 3 hours

Specialty equipment
Cleaver
Tamis or fine mesh strainer
Deep fryer
Gnocchi board (optional)

Gnocchi
2 lb **golden fleshed potatoes**
1½ cups **all-purpose flour** + more for dusting
2 tsp **salt**
1 **egg yolk**, room temperature

Finishing the Plate
Crispy potato skins
Sour cream
Green onions, sliced
Parmesan cheese, grated

Glace de Viande
Neck and carcass from 1 chicken
1 tbsp **duck fat**
2 **shallots**
1 **stick celery**
1 **carrot**
1 tsp **tomato paste**
1 cup **white wine**
8 cups **ChickenStock** (recipe on page 91)
½ tsp **black peppercorns**
1 **bay leaf**

FOR THE GLACE DE VIANDE

Cut the bones into smaller pieces using a large knife or cleaver. You can also ask your butcher to do this for you.

Add the duck fat to a saucepot on high heat.

Add the chicken bones and sear them golden brown on all sides. Use long tongs to turn to rotate the bones; the oil may spit a little from the water in the bones. Remove the bones and set aside.

Add the shallots, carrots, and celery to the pot. Cook the vegetables, stirring occasionally until they start to caramelize.

Place the bones back into the pot. Add the tomato paste and stir.

Next, deglaze with white wine and cook until the wine has almost completely evaporated.

Add the chicken stock, peppercorns, and bay leaf. Turn the heat down to a low simmer.

Skim any impurities that come to the surface while the sauce is reducing.

Cook until it has a saucy consistency and has reduced by three quarters. Prepare your gnocchi while the sauce reduces.

FOR THE GNOCCHI

Preheat oven to 375°F.

Put a thin layer of salt on a baking tray.

Wash and dry the potatoes and bake them on the bed of salt for 1½–2 hours, until the potatoes are fork-tender. Remove the potatoes from the oven.

Wear a pair of gloves to work with the potatoes. They must remain hot until they are mixed so that your gnocchi do not have a gluey texture.

Brush the salt off the potatoes. Cut them in half and scoop out the flesh with a spoon, leaving a thin layer of potato in the shell. Set the shells aside.

Press the potato flesh through a tamis or fine mesh strainer into a bowl.

Add in the flour, salt, and egg yolk. Mix the dough gently until it just comes together. The dough should feel like firm mashed potatoes.

Turn the dough out onto a floured work surface.

Cut a ¼ of the dough and roll it into a thin log.

Cut the log into ½-inch pieces. Using your hands, square off the edges of each piece and place the gnocchi onto a floured tray. Store the gnocchi in the freezer.

FINISHING THE PLATE

Preheat a deep fryer to 350°F.

Cut the potato skins into smaller pieces. Drop into the fryer and cook the potato skins until golden brown and crispy, about 2 minutes.

Remove from the fryer and season with salt.

Boil a pot of heavily salted water. Add the gnocchi in batches so the water continues to boil.

Cook until the gnocchi float to the surface. Remove the gnocchi and add them to a large frying pan.

Strain the sauce and place it into the frying pan. Toss the sauce and gnocchi together.

Divide the gnocchi onto plates and garnish them with crispy potato skins, sour cream, green onion, and parmesan cheese.

CHEF NOTES

Try adding some crispy Maple Bacon (recipe on page 23) to this dish!

You may also want to make traditionally shaped gnocchi using a gnocchi board. Press the pieces of dough lightly across the board to create cylindrical gnocchi with ridges designed to hold sauce.

The small towns of Blanes and Vic, Spain

Meat and Fish

In a professional kitchen, the meat station is one of the most crucial, where timing is everything. Meats and fish must be cooked to perfection, hot, and in some cases, rested to the required doneness just in time to send to the table. In a restaurant, more experienced cooks are typically required to butcher and cook meat and fish. In this chapter, I share a few of my favourite crowd-pleasing dishes that are easy to make at home.

Crispy Calamari with Aji Amarillo Aioli

Crispy fried squid, also known as calamari, is a popular dish in Mediterranean cuisine and is typically enjoyed as an appetizer or shared plate. The secret to giving calamari an extra bit of crunchiness in this recipe is the rice that's added into the flour dredge. I enjoy the texture and crunch when the calamari is hot out of the fryer!

The *aji amarillo* aioli dip has just the right amount of spice and it pairs well with the delicate, sweet flavour of the squid. Aji amarillo peppers are a spicy, small yellow-orange pepper with a fruity sweet flavour, commonly used in Peruvian cuisine. The heat from the peppers is medium but does not leave your mouth burning as some other chili peppers do.

Yield: Serves 4–6
Preparation time: 1½–2 hours
Cook time: 25 minutes

Specialty equipment
Fine mesh strainer
Blender
Food processor
Deep fryer

Aji Amarillo Aioli

2 **egg yolks**
2 tbsp **aji amarillo pepper paste**
1 **clove garlic**, chopped
1 tbsp **white vinegar**
½ tsp **salt**
1 cup **canola oil**

Calamari

10 oz **baby squid tubes and tentacles**
½ cup **whole milk**
Green onion
Espelette pepper flakes

Dry Dredge

¼ cup **rice**
½ cup **flour**
2 tbsp **cornstarch**
1 tsp **salt**
½ tsp **fresh cracked black pepper**
¼ tsp **onion powder**

FOR THE AIOLI

Place all the ingredients except the oil into a food processor and turn it on.

Slowly add the canola oil until the mixture has become emulsified, thick, and creamy.

Store the aioli in a container with a tight-fitting lid in the refrigerator. It will keep for about one week.

FOR THE DREDGE

Place the rice into a blender and purée it into a fine powder. I used carnaroli rice, but any type of white rice will work. Alternatively, you may want to use store-bought white rice flour.

Sift the rice through a fine mesh strainer to remove any large pieces. Mix the powdered rice with flour, salt, pepper, and onion powder.

FOR THE CALAMARI

Preheat a deep fryer to 350°F.

To clean the whole squid, separate the head and tentacles from the body by grasping both ends and pulling to separate.

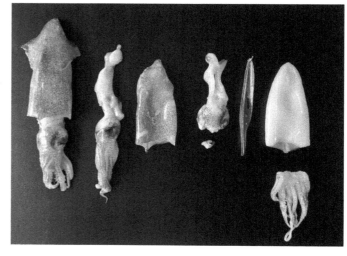

Cut the head off the squid tentacles. Make a small cut on one side to remove the beak from the centre of the tentacles.

Clean out the inside of the tube body. There is a clear piece of cartilage that is easily removed. The spotted skin also separates easily from the outside of the body.

Rinse the squid thoroughly under cold water and pat dry.

Cut the tubes into rings. The body and tentacles are now ready to use.

Pour the milk into a container and add the squid. Let them soak for 5 minutes.

Take the squid out of the milk. Place in the dredge, coating the squid evenly. Shake off any excess.

Drop squid into the deep fryer. Cook in batches to make sure the fryer doesn't cool and make your calamari greasy. Squid can also overcook quickly and become chewy.

Remove the calamari from the fryer when it is golden brown and crispy, about 3 minutes. Toss it with espelette pepper flakes and garnish with green onion.

Serve the calamari with aji amarillo aioli dip.

CHEF NOTES

You may want to ask your fishmonger to clean the squid for you. Alternatively, you can buy the squid already cleaned and cut into rings.

Steelhead Trout En Papillote

En papillote is French for "enveloped in paper," a cooking method where the food is wrapped up like a parcel, typically with parchment paper, and baked. For this recipe, I have used a transparent cooking film called carta fata, which can withstand baking temperatures above 400°F.

Steelhead trout is an orange-fleshed fish like salmon but with a milder flavour. Poached with deliciously seasoned vegetables and enrobed in a tangy shallot beurre blanc, the steelhead trout becomes moist, tender, and flakey when it is cooked en papillote. You may also want to try salmon or prawns, substituting different vegetables with a cream sauce or with stock for a healthy option.

Yield: Serves 4
Preparation time: 2 hours
Cook time: 1 hour

4 x 5-oz portions **fresh steelhead trout**
   skin removed

Beurre Blanc
⅓ cup **shallot**, brunoised
½ cup **dry white wine**
Pinch **xanthan gum**
1 cup **cold salted butter**, cut into cubes

Specialty equipment
Carta fata paper;
   alternatively, you can use parchment paper
Butchers' twine

Vegetables
1 large **zucchini**, turned
2 **carrots**, batonnet
2 cups **cauliflower florets**
2 cups **broccoli florets**

Wrapping the Fish
4, 20 x 24-inch pieces of carta fata wrap
Fresh dill for garnish

FOR THE BEURRE BLANC

Place the shallots and white wine in a small pot on medium heat. Cook until the wine has reduced by half.

Reduce the heat to low and whisk in the xanthan gum. The xanthan gum is used to stabilize the sauce so that when it is baked the butter doesn't split and become greasy.

Continue whisking and add in the butter a few cubes at a time, letting it melt in between additions.

Check the temperature of the butter sauce to make sure it stays warm but not hot. Remove the pot from the heat and keep whisking in cold butter if it gets too hot.

FOR THE VEGETABLES

Fill a saucepot with water and salt and turn it on high heat.

Blanch the broccoli, carrots, and cauliflower separately in the boiling water until they are tender but still have bite to them, about 2 minutes each.

Remove the vegetables from the water directly into an ice bath to cool. Then place them onto a towel-lined tray to dry.

Sauté the zucchini in a frying pan on high heat with a small amount of oil. Cook until the zucchini starts to brown on both sides. Turn off the heat and set aside.

WRAPPING THE FISH

Preheat oven to 350°F.

Season the steelhead trout with salt on both sides.

Heat a frying pan on high and add the trout. Sear the fish for 1 minute on each side to add colour but not to cook the fish through.

Remove the fish onto a tray. Cool it in the refrigerator.

Set the carta fata paper on a pie plate and arrange the vegetables in a circle.

Place the steelhead in the centre and spoon the beurre blanc over the fish.

Bundle up the carta fata paper and tie it with butchers' twine. Cut away any excess paper to make a tidy parcel.

Set packages on a baking sheet and cook in the oven for 15–20 minutes.

Serve the fish immediately. Simply place the packages in a bowl, open, and garnish with fresh dill.

CHEF NOTES

The packages can be made a day or two ahead. Store in the refrigerator and bake when you are ready to serve.

Sablefish Marinated with White Miso

Sablefish is a white-fleshed deep-sea fish commonly found in the north of the Pacific Ocean. Also referred to as butterfish, its soft, flaky texture is rich and savoury when cooked. For this recipe, I have marinated the fish in white miso, a salty fermented soybean seasoning traditionally used in Japanese cuisine.

I love the pairings of the salty miso with the richness of the sablefish. The tart, floral notes of grapefruit, and earthy undertones of the mushrooms, beans, and leeks combine to make this dish pleasantly balanced and appetizing.

Yield: Serves 4
Preparation time: 1½ hours + overnight
Cook time: 1½ hours

4 x 6-oz portions of **sablefish**

Miso Marinade
½ cup **white miso**
2 tbsp **mirin**
1½ tbsp **sugar**
1 tsp **rice vinegar**
½ tsp **salt**

Grapefruit
1 **ruby red grapefruit**, segmented
Juice from the grapefruit
2 tsp **mirin**
1 tsp **sugar**

Finishing the Plate
4 **king oyster mushrooms**
½ cup **butter**
2 tbsp **canola oil**
2 cups **romano green beans**
2 cups **leeks**

FOR THE SABLEFISH

Mix the miso, mirin, vinegar, sugar, and salt in a bowl.

Rub the fish portions all over with the marinade.

Place the marinated fish onto a baking tray. Wrap and refrigerate overnight.

FOR THE GRAPEFRUIT

Preheat oven to 225°F.

Using a sharp paring knife, peel the grapefruit, making sure to remove all the pith.

Cut out the fruit segments and place them into a mixing bowl.

Squeeze any excess juice from the pith in with the segments and mix with the sugar and mirin.

Place the grapefruit segments onto a baking tray lined with parchment paper and into the oven for approximately 1½ hours. Brush them every 15 minutes with the juice from the bowl until they are slightly dried and start to become sticky.

FINISHING THE PLATE

Preheat the broiler in an oven on high.

Cut the king oyster mushrooms in half. Use the tip of a sharp paring knife to score the inside flesh of the mushrooms.

Put 2 tablespoons of butter and 1 tablespoon of oil into a frying pan on high heat.

Add the mushrooms, scored side down, and sear until they become golden brown.

Turn the mushrooms over. Using a large spoon, baste the mushrooms with the butter, adding more butter if needed. Cook until the mushrooms are soft and nicely seared all over.

Remove the mushrooms from the heat, and season with salt and pepper.

Cut the leeks and beans on a bias, creating a diamond-shaped cut in each vegetable.

Fill a small pot with salted water and bring it to a boil on high heat. Add the beans and blanch for 2 minutes. Remove them immediately and plunge into an ice bath. Strain the beans when cooled and pat them dry.

In a large frying pan, heat 2 tablespoons butter and 1 tablespoon oil on high heat.

Add the leeks to the pan and sauté for about 2 minutes, stirring for even cooking.

Add the blanched beans and cook for about 5 minutes until the vegetables are heated through.

Put the fish onto a new baking tray lined with parchment paper and cook under the broiler for 10–12 minutes. The marinade will start to brown and become caramelized. Remove the fish from the oven.

Plate the fish with the mushrooms, leeks, and beans, garnish with the grapefruit, and a drizzle of the grapefruit juice.

CHEF NOTES

You may also want to try scallops in the miso marinade. Or for a vegetarian meal, try using cauliflower or eggplant marinated and then roasted.

Chicken Stock

This is how I always make chicken stock at home. I slowly simmer a whole chicken with vegetables, herbs, and spices until the meat is tender and falls off the bone. Then the chicken meat can be pulled and made into the most delicious chicken soup or for the **Chicken Pot Pie** recipe on page 95.

Cooking low and slow is key to not drying out the chicken meat. In this recipe, I have used a whole chicken, with feet and head still intact. The feet and neck are best for adding gelatin and collagen to the stock that will later produce a rich and flavourful sauce.

Yield: **12 cups**
Preparation time: **45 minutes**
Cook time: **2½ hours**

Specialty equipment
Cleaver
8-quart stockpot
Fine mesh strainer

1 **whole chicken**
1⅓ gallons **cold water**
1 **onion**
2 small **carrots**
2 sticks of **celery**

1 **Roma tomato**
1 bunch **parsley**, stems only
3 sprigs of **fresh thyme**
4 **bay leaves**
1 tsp **black peppercorns**

FOR THE STOCK

Separate the head and feet from the body of the chicken using a large chef knife or cleaver.

Put the pieces with the chicken in an 8-quart stockpot. Cover it with cold water and place it on the stove over medium heat.

Peel and chop the onions, carrots, celery, and tomato into smaller pieces and set them aside with the rest of the ingredients.

As the water heats, use a ladle to skim off the scum that floats to the surface.

As soon as the water starts to boil, turn the heat to a low simmer.

Add the rest of the ingredients and cook for 2 hours.

Turn the heat off. Allow the chicken to cool completely in the stock and place it in the refrigerator overnight.

Remove the chicken and strain the stock through a fine mesh strainer. Your chicken stock is ready for use and can be stored for a week in the fridge. The stock also freezes well for later use.

CHEF NOTES

I use this chicken stock for braising meats and for the glace de viande in the gnocchi recipe on page 77.

Chicken Pot Pie

One of the ultimate comfort foods for me is chicken pot pie. Tender chunks of braised chicken and caramelized vegetables are simmered in rich chicken gravy, accented with fresh herbs, and baked in a melt-in-your-mouth buttery, flaky pastry.

I use the **Chicken Stock Recipe** (page 91) for the braised chicken and use the stock to make the gravy, which adds fullness to the flavour and texture. There's no better way to warm up on a snowy day in Calgary.

Yield: 10 x 5-inch pies
Preparation time: 2–3 hours
Cook time: 1½–2 hours

Specialty equipment
Ring cutters
5-inch pie tins

Pot Pie Filling
1½ lb **cooked chicken meat**
1 cup **yellow onion**
1 cup **carrot**
1 cup **celery**
3 tbsp **canola oil**
5 cloves **garlic**, chopped
¾ cup **sweet peas**
½ cup **parmesan cheese, grated**
¼ cup **chives, chopped**

Gravy
5 cups **chicken stock**
3½ oz **butter**
3½ oz **flour**
1 tbsp **fresh thyme leaves**
3 tsp **salt**
1 tsp **fresh cracked black pepper**

Pie Shells
Pastry Dough
(recipe on page 119)

Finishing the Pies
2 **eggs**, beaten

FOR THE FILLING

Cut the chicken meat into small pieces and add it to a large mixing bowl.

Dice the onions, carrots, and celery and keep them separate from each other.

Add a tablespoon of oil to a frying pan on medium heat. Add the onions to the pan and cook until they start to brown.

Add the garlic, cook for about a minute, then remove the onions and garlic from the pan.

Place another tablespoon of oil into the frying pan and sauté the carrots, then the celery, separately, until they are tender but still have bite to them.

Allow the vegetables to cool. Add them with the rest of the filling ingredients to the bowl with the chicken meat and set it aside in the refrigerator while you prepare the gravy.

FOR THE GRAVY

Heat the stock in a saucepot on high heat.

Melt the butter in a separate pot on high heat.

Add the flour to the melted butter and cook the roux until it resembles white sand.

Turn the heat to medium and start adding the hot stock, a cup at a time, whisking until smooth after each addition.

Add the fresh thyme leaves and cook the gravy, whisking occasionally, for 15 minutes. Turn off the heat, season with salt and pepper, and pour the gravy into a container to cool.

Pour the gravy into the bowl with the vegetables and chicken meat and mix to combine.

FOR THE PIE SHELLS

Cut the pastry dough in two, rolling out one half at a time to make it easier to work with. Roll dough to about a ¼-inch thick.

Cut 10, 7-inch rounds for the pie shell bottoms and 10, 5-inch rounds for the tops.

FINISHING THE PIES

Preheat oven to 375°F.

Press the bottom rounds of dough into the 5-inch pie plates. Make sure to press the dough down snug into the pan and leave about a ½ inch of dough hanging over the edge.

Add ¾ of a cup of filling to each pie.

Brush the edges with egg.

Add the top dough, crimp the edges closed, and brush the tops with more egg.

Bake in the oven for 40–50 minutes until the pies are golden brown. The raw pies can also be frozen for later use.

CHEF NOTES

To keep the pastry dough as cold as possible while you assemble the pies, place them on a tray in the refrigerator while you are sealing each top. Chill the pies for 30 minutes before baking, this will turn out a flakier crust.

Pork Ribs with Quince Glaze

Quince is a fruit that's golden yellow when ripe. It has a fragrant aroma and is shaped like a cross between an apple and a pear. Quince is typically used to make jams, jellies, marmalades, and desserts because of its high level of natural pectin. The pulp is simmered slowly, turning it dark burgundy in colour, and has a sweet, slightly astringent flavour.

I have used quince paste in this recipe to create a sweet and sour glaze that complements the rich fattiness of the pork ribs. Serve these sweet and savoury ribs as an appetizer or paired with your favourite coleslaw or potato salad.

Yield: 1 rack of baby back ribs
Preparation time: 1 hour
Cook time: 4 hours

Specialty equipment
Dutch oven
Mandolin
Fine mesh strainer

Pork Ribs
1 **rack of baby back pork ribs**
1 tbsp **salt**
1 **onion**
1 stick **celery**
⅓ cup **fresh ginger,** chopped
3 **bay leaves**
1 tsp **peppercorns**
8 cups **Chicken Stock** (recipe page 91)

Garlic Chips
3 large **cloves of garlic**
2 tbsp **canola oil**

Quince Glaze
½ cup **quince paste**
3 tsp **hot smoked paprika**
½ cup **red wine vinegar**
1 tsp **garlic powder**
¼ cup **honey**
1 tsp **salt**
2 tbsp **fresh parsley**, chopped for garnish

BRAISING THE RIBS

Preheat oven to 285°F.

Remove the membrane from the rib side of the rack. This is the thin layer of tissue that easily pulls away from the bone. Discard.

Season the ribs generously on both sides with salt.

Cut the onion, celery, and ginger into smaller pieces. Add them to a Dutch oven with bay leaves, peppercorns, chicken stock, and ribs.

Turn the pot on high heat and bring it to a boil.

Turn the heat off, cover the pot with a tight-fitting lid, and cook in the oven for 3 hours.

Remove the ribs from the oven, remove the lid, and allow them to cool completely in the braising liquid.

FOR THE GARLIC CHIPS

Set up a fine mesh strainer over a mixing bowl.

Peel the garlic cloves and slice, about ⅛-inch thick, using a mandolin.

Add the garlic and canola oil into a non-stick frying pan over medium heat.

Cook the garlic until it just starts to turn light golden brown. Stir continuously for even browning.

Turn off the heat and strain the garlic immediately through the fine mesh strainer to stop cooking.

The oil can be used again for garlic chips or in other recipes for a hint of roasted garlic flavour.

FOR THE QUINCE GLAZE

Whisk all the ingredients in a small pot on high heat.

Bring to a boil. Cook the sauce for 2 minutes, then turn off the heat.

Remove the ribs from the braising liquid and place them onto a tray lined with parchment paper, rib side up.

Cook the ribs under a broiler for 5–7 minutes until they start to get golden and crispy.

Brush the ribs with half of the glaze and broil for another 7 minutes.

Turn the ribs meat side up, brush with the rest of the glaze, and cook until they start to caramelize, 5–8 minutes.

Garnish the ribs with crispy garlic chips and fresh chopped parsley.

CHEF NOTES

Strain the braising liquid and save it for the next time you make ribs.

Cider-Braised Pork Shoulder Lettuce Wraps

I love braising meat, cooking it low and slow to the perfect, juicy, fall-off-the-bone doneness. For this braised pork shoulder, I have included dry apple cider and porcini mushrooms, to bring both earthy and savoury notes to the dish. I use a Dutch oven for braising, but a slow cooker would also work well for this recipe. Set in the morning and the pork will be ready for dinner.

Pork shoulder is a large whole muscle, so salting it and allowing it to sit for a few hours (usually overnight) in the refrigerator before cooking will ensure that the meat comes out perfectly seasoned throughout.

Yield: Serves 6–8
Preparation time: 2 hours + overnight
Cook time: 8 hours

Braised Pork Shoulder
4½ lb **pork shoulder**, bone-in
Salt
2 tbsp **canola oil**
1 **yellow onion**, diced
1 **gala apple,** peeled and diced
1 cup **celery**, chopped
6 cloves **garlic**, chopped
1 cup **apple cider**
½ oz **dried porcini mushrooms**
1 tbsp **thyme leaves**
4 bay **leaves**
1 tsp **fresh cracked black pepper**
4 cups **pork stock**

Specialty equipment
Dutch oven or slow cooker

Lettuce Wraps
Butterleaf lettuce
Shaved onion
Italian flat-leaf parsley
Fresh cilantro
Chilis
Hot Sauce (see recipe on page 13)
Pickled Fennel (see recipe on page 19)

BRAISING THE PORK

Season the pork shoulder generously with salt. Allow it to sit overnight in the refrigerator.

Preheat oven to 285°F.

Add the oil to a Dutch oven and turn it on high heat.

Sauté the onions, celery, and garlic until they start to brown.

Deglaze the pot with the apple cider.

Add the rest of the ingredients to the pot with the salted pork shoulder.

Bring the stock to a boil, turn the heat off, add a tight-fitting lid, and cook in the oven for 8 hours.

Remove the pork from the oven and leave it to rest in the braise for 30 minutes.

Remove the shoulder from the braising liquid.

Simmer the braising liquid on medium heat to reduce it slightly. Use a ladle to skim the fat off the top. Discard.

Put the shoulder back into the sauce to heat it through.

FINISHING THE LETTUCE WRAPS

Serve the pork with the accompaniments. I like to wrap a bit of the pulled pork shoulder with shaved onion, parsley, cilantro, a few chilis, pickled fennel, and a bit of hot sauce in the butterleaf lettuce.

CHEF NOTES

Serve over rice, potatoes, or pasta as another dinner option for the braised pork shoulder.

You could try using the braising liquid from the Pork Ribs on (page 97) as the pork stock for this recipe.

Beer-Braised Beef Short Ribs and Chanterelles

Braising is a method of cooking that uses both wet and dry heat. In this recipe, the short ribs are grilled, rather than pan-seared before braising the meat. This adds the noteworthy flavour and aroma of charred beef to the final braise. If you enjoy cooking over an open fire, this recipe will be the perfect opportunity to do so and will add a smoky element to the meat, which pairs beautifully with chanterelle mushrooms.

Yield: Serves 4 people
Preparation time: 1 hour
Cook time: 3½ hours

Specialty equipment
Dutch oven

Braised Short Rib
3 lb **bone-in beef short ribs**
Salt
Fresh cracked black pepper
2 **yellow onions**
¼ cup **canola oil**
4 cloves **garlic**
1 cup **brown ale**
1 **Roma tomato**
1 tbsp **fresh thyme leaves**
1 tbsp **fresh rosemary**, stems removed
3 **bay leaves**
1 tbsp Pickled Mustard Seeds
(recipe on page 17)
4 cups Chicken Stock (recipe page 91)

Finishing the Plate
2 tbsp **butter**
2 tsp **canola oil**
½ lb **fresh chanterelle mushrooms**
Italian flat-leaf parsley
Pinch of **salt and pepper**

FOR THE SHORT RIB

Preheat a grill on high and oven to 285°F.

Season the short ribs liberally with salt and pepper and allow them to sit while you prepare the aromatics.

Julienne the onions and add them to a Dutch oven with the canola oil.

Cook the onions on medium heat, stirring occasionally until they become caramelized.

Add the garlic and cook for 1 minute, stirring continuously.

Deglaze with the brown ale and cook until the beer has almost completely evaporated.

Add the rest of the ingredients except the short ribs and turn the heat down to low.

Grill the short ribs on all sides and add them to the pot.

Cover and place it in the oven for 3 hours.

Remove the pot from the oven and remove the lid. Allow the short ribs to rest in the braising liquid for at least 30 minutes.

Remove the short ribs from the braise and set aside. Place the pot on medium heat and reduce it by half. The liquid will have a sauce-like consistency.

Divide the short ribs into four portions, then add them back to the sauce to heat them through.

FINISHING THE PLATE

In a large frying pan on high heat, melt the butter and oil together.

Add the chanterelle mushrooms and sauté, stirring occasionally until they are golden brown.

Turn off the heat, add the fresh parsley leaves and season with salt and pepper.

Place a piece of short rib onto a plate with a spoonful of sauce.

Add the chanterelle mushrooms and serve.

CHEF NOTES

Try this braising technique using different cuts of meat, vegetables, and aromatics such as red wine instead of beer.

Wagyu Striploin with Red Chimichurri

Wagyu is a Japanese breed of cattle known for its extensive marbling produced by the process in which the cattle are raised. Wagyu cows are pampered in comparison to mass-produced cattle. They are fed a special diet and given more space both in and out of their pens to graze freely in a low-stress environment.

Wagyu beef is incredibly buttery and tender when it is cooked, making it one of the most sought-after and expensive meats. I like to serve this rich, luxurious beef as a shared steak, paired with my red version of chimichurri sauce and sauteed broccolini.

Yield: Serves 1–3
Preparation time: 1½ hour
Cook time: 45 minutes

1 x 10-oz **Japanese Wagyu striploin**
Salt

Red Chimichurri

1 **red bell pepper**, finely diced
2½ oz **piquillo peppers**, finely diced
2 cloves **garlic,** minced
1 **shallot,** finely diced
¼ cup **olive oil**
2 tbsp sherry vinegar
1 tbsp **cilantro, chopped**
1 tsp **smoked paprika**
1 tsp **salt**

Sautéed Broccolini

½ lb **broccolini**
1 large **shallot**, julienned
Salt

FOR THE CHIMICHURRI

Combine all the ingredients in a mixing bowl. Set aside.

FOR THE BROCCOLINI

Fill a saucepot with water and salt and bring it to a boil. The water should taste a bit salty for perfectly seasoned broccolini.

Blanch the broccolini for 3 minutes.

Remove the broccolini and place it into an ice bath to cool. Transfer to a towel to dry and set aside.

FINISHING THE PLATE

Heat a frying pan on high heat.

Season the steak on all sides with salt.

Once the pan is hot, sear the steak for about a minute on each side.

Turn the heat down to medium, keeping the pan hot but not burning the steak.

Take the pan away from the heat, remove the steak, and let it rest for 5 minutes.

Place the pan back on the heat. Once it is hot again, sear the steak again for about 1 minute per side.

The steak should have a golden-brown crust. I like it to be cooked medium, which allows the fat to warm sufficiently and become melt in your mouth buttery and tender.

Use this technique to cook the steak but adjust the cooking time depending on how thick the steak is cut.

Remove the steak and allow it to rest for 5 minutes.

Add the julienne shallots and blanched broccolini to the pan on medium heat.

Sauté for about 5 minutes and season with salt and pepper to taste.

Serve the steak cut into pieces with the chimichurri sauce and broccolini.

CHEF NOTES

Try this recipe with ribeye steak instead of wagyu, adjust the cooking time for the desired doneness.

Notes

Fresh produce market in Blanes, Spain

Mercado de La Boqueria in Barcelona

Sweets and Treats

For my final chapter, I combine cheese, pastries, and desserts with a few of my favourite beverages. The dessert station in a restaurant can include an array of items, savoury or sweet. Think of dishes such as cheese plates, crackers, or freshly baked breads. Sweet desserts, cakes, and pastries accompanied by fruit, chocolate, or cookie garnishes and beautifully presented. I have added a few techniques I have learned that are fun to try at home.

Honey-Roasted Figs and Ricotta Cheese
Passionfruit Panna Cotta with Aerated
Coconut Cake
Pastry Dough
Faux Apple Pies
Churros with Lime and Dulce de Leche

Strawberry and Cream Terrarium
Pumpkin Sticky Toffee Pudding
Vermouth
Yuzu Jalapeño Lemonade
Sangria
Chanterelle Mushroom-Infused Vodka Caesar

Honey-Roasted Figs and Ricotta Cheese

A baguette topped with honey-roasted figs and ricotta cheese will work perfectly as either an appetizer or served at the end of the meal as a sweet yet savoury cheese course.

I've chosen ricotta cheese for this dish because of its subtle, sweet flavour and creamy texture. It will accent the sweetness of the figs, and it is incredibly easy to make at home! Introducing an acid—such as lemon juice or vinegar—to warm milk and cream will separate the milk and cream into soft curds and whey.

Figs have a mild, floral, honey-like flavour that becomes more intense when roasted. The combined flavours of honey-roasted figs, creamy ricotta cheese, and tangy walnut vinaigrette served on a fresh baguette will be a delicious part of your meal.

Yield: Serves 6–8
Preparation time: 1 hour + overnight
Cook time: 1 hour

Ricotta
2 cups **whole milk**
1 cup **heavy cream**
¼ tsp **salt**
1 tbsp **white vinegar**

Roasted Figs
17 **fresh black figs**
3 tbsp **honey**
1 tbsp **water**
Pinch of **salt**

Specialty equipment
Thermometer
Fine mesh strainer

Walnut Vinaigrette
Syrup from roasting the figs
½ cup **walnuts**
2 tbsp **walnut oil**
3 tsp **sherry vinegar**
¼ tsp **salt**

Finishing the Plate
1 fresh **baguette**

FOR THE RICOTTA

Heat the milk, cream, and salt together on high heat, stirring constantly until the temperature reaches between 185°F and 190°F.

Add the vinegar; stir and remove the pot from the heat.

Put a tight-fitting lid on the pot and let it sit for 15 minutes.

Using a slotted spoon, remove the curds into a draining basket or fine mesh strainer lined with cheesecloth and allow the liquid to drain in the refrigerator overnight.

FOR THE ROASTED FIGS

Preheat oven to 375°F.

Put 15 of the figs onto a 6 x 10-inch baking tray. Set aside the other 2 figs for garnish later.

Drizzle the figs with honey and a pinch of salt then add water to the bottom of the tray.

Bake in the oven for 35 minutes. Use a large spoon to baste them with the liquid from the pan every 10 minutes.

Remove the figs from the oven and set them aside to cool.

FOR THE WALNUT VINAIGRETTE

Drain the syrup from the figs into a mixing bowl.

Add the walnuts to a baking tray and toast them in the same oven as the figs for 5–10 minutes, until they are golden brown.

Take the walnuts out of the oven and into the mixing bowl with the rest of the ingredients.

FINISHING THE PLATE

Cut the baguette into ½-inch thick slices.

Spread some of the ricotta cheese on each slice and place them onto a serving platter.

Top with the roasted figs, slices of fresh fig, and drizzled with the walnut vinaigrette.

CHEF NOTES

Try using roasted pears for this recipe when figs are out of season.

Passionfruit Panna Cotta with Aerated Coconut Cake

Panna cotta is an Italian dessert made from sweetened heavy cream thickened with gelatin, then infused or garnished with your favourite flavours and toppings. For this recipe, I will infuse the panna cotta with passionfruit purée and add the lightest coconut cake you'll ever experience, then garnish with fresh passionfruit and raspberries for a colourfully divine dessert.

This panna cotta recipe is quick to make but will taste like you've spent hours preparing it. The passionfruit, which is delightfully floral as well as sweet with a subtle tartness, pairs well with coconut. My coconut cake recipe uses only six ingredients, which are combined and dispensed from an iSi canister and baked for less than a minute in the microwave.

Yield: Serves 4
Preparation time: 1 hour + overnight
Cook time: 15 minutes

Specialty equipment
Fine mesh strainer
iSi canister + N_2O charges

Panna Cotta
3 **gelatin sheets** (6 g)
1 cup **passionfruit purée**
½ cup **heavy cream**
½ cup **sugar**
1 cup **whole milk**
fresh passionfruit and **raspberries** for garnish

Aerated Coconut Cake
2 **eggs**
3 tbsp **coconut milk**
3 ½ tbsp **all-purpose flour**
3 tbsp **coconut oil**, melted
1 ½ tbsp **sugar**
½ tsp **salt**
4 x 5-oz paper cups for microwaving

FOR THE PANNA COTTA

Set up a fine mesh strainer over a mixing bowl.

In a small bowl, soak the gelatin sheets in cold water to soften.

Mix the passionfruit purée, heavy cream, and sugar in a small pot and turn it on high heat.

Stir continuously until the mixture comes to a boil. Remove from the heat.

Take the gelatin sheets out of the water and squeeze out any excess. Whisk them into the passionfruit mix. Strain the mix through the fine mesh strainer.

In a separate mixing bowl, add the milk. While whisking, slowly add the passionfruit mix to the milk to temper it. If the passionfruit mix is added too quickly, it could separate the milk.

Divide the mixture evenly into four bowls and place them in the refrigerator overnight to set.

FOR THE CAKE

Whisk all ingredients together in a mixing bowl. Pour the mixture into an iSi canister and dispense two N_2O cartridges into it.

Using a sharp knife, poke many small holes into the paper cups.

Give the canister a good shake and fill one cup halfway with the cake batter.

Bake it in the microwave for 55 seconds on high.

Remove the cake from the microwave and let it cool while you repeat with the rest of the cups.

Carefully remove the cakes once they have cooled. Serve them immediately as a garnish for the panna cotta, topped with fresh passionfruit and raspberries.

CHEF NOTES

When all the cake batter has been dispensed from the iSi canister, release any extra gas from inside over a sink before opening it.

Pastry Dough

This pastry recipe is versatile and easy to make turning out a rich, buttery, and flakey crust. Use this pastry dough for hand pies, traditional pies, and tarts. It works perfectly with both sweet and savoury fillings; I use it also for the **Chicken Pot Pies** on (page 95).

Yield: 2 lb
Preparation time: 20 minutes + overnight

3 cups **all-purpose flour**
¼ tsp **salt**
¾ lb **salted butter**
1 cup **cold water**

FOR THE PASTRY DOUGH

Combine the flour and salt in a large mixing bowl.

Cut the butter into small pieces and add it to the flour mix.

Using your hands, press the mix into smaller, flattened pieces. This will help create layers in your pastry dough that become flaky when baked.

Add the cold water and mix until the dough just starts to come together, folding it into itself to create layers in the pastry.

Wrap the dough and refrigerate for at least 2 hours or overnight for best results.

CHEF NOTES

Refrigerate all the ingredients for this recipe. The colder the dough is when mixed, the flakier your pastry will be.

Faux Apple Pie

The first time John made this dessert for me, I couldn't believe it wasn't apple pie. I enjoy experimenting with vegetables in dessert dishes. I find that they've been underrated and there are, in fact, many vegetables that can be turned into sweet treats.

Eggplant, by botanical definition, is a berry, but it is commonly used as a vegetable in cooking. Eggplant has a neutral flavour, and it acts like a sponge, soaking up the flavours of the other ingredients in the dish, which makes it the perfect ingredient to try in a dessert recipe. Choose a firm eggplant to help replicate the texture of cooked apples in apple pie. The malic and citric acids add flavour and acidity, so it tastes like an apple, but the secret is in the recipe.

Yield: 6 x 4-inch pies
Preparation time: 2–3 hours
Cook time: 45 minutes

Specialty equipment
4-inch fluted tart shells
Ring cutters

Pie Filling
½ cup + 2 tbsp **butter**
1 lb **eggplant**
1 cup **brown sugar**, packed
½ tsp **cinnamon**
¼ tsp **salt**
¼ cup **water**
¼ tsp **malic acid**
⅛ tsp **citric acid**

Pie Crust
½ **Pastry Dough** recipe on (page 119)

FOR THE PIE FILLING

Peel the eggplant and dice it small.

Melt half a cup of butter in a large saucepot on high heat.

Add the eggplant to the pan and sauté, stirring occasionally. Place a lid on the pot in between stirring to slightly steam the eggplant.

Once the eggplant is cooked, 8–10 minutes, turn the heat down and add the brown sugar, cinnamon, salt, water, and 2 tablespoons of butter. Cook for about 3 more minutes.

Remove the eggplant from the heat. Stir in the malic and citric acids.

Allow the filling to cool completely while you prepare the pastry for the pies.

ROLLING THE PASTRY

Preheat oven to 375°F.

Roll the dough out a ¼ inch thick.

Cut 5-inch rounds for the bottoms of the pies and six 4-inch rounds for the tops.

Using six 4-inch fluted tart shells sprayed with non-stick spray, press the bottom rounds of dough into the pie plates.

Fill each with ¼ cup of eggplant filling.

Cut the top rounds of pastry dough into strips. Brush them lightly with beaten egg and create a lattice on the top of the pies.

Chill the pies for 30 minutes then bake them in the oven for 20–25 minutes until the pastry is golden brown.

Remove the pies from the oven. Let them cool slightly and serve on their own or with a scoop of vanilla ice cream.

CHEF NOTES

Try substituting apple for the eggplant in this recipe for a more traditional treat.

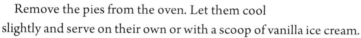

Churros with Lime and Dulce de Leche

Churros bring back exciting memories of a carnival in Bermeo, a picturesque little town nestled in the northern Basque region of Spain. The smell of sweet, deep-fried dough dusted with cinnamon and served piled high in a paper cup, crispy and soft, is simple perfection.

For this recipe, I will roll the fried churros in lime sugar and serve them with whipped dulce de leche. When I first learned this technique, I was amazed that simply boiling a can of sweetened condensed milk for several hours will turn the contents into a lusciously thick dark caramel known as dulce de leche. The savoury hint of lime on the churros pairs well with the rich, sweet dulce de leche.

Yield: 8–10 churros
Preparation time: 25 minutes
Cook time: 6–8 hours + overnight

Specialty equipment
Stand mixer
Piping bag + star piping tip
Deep fryer

Dulce de Leche
1 can **sweetened condensed milk**

Churros
¾ cup **water**
2 tbsp **butter**
½ tsp **salt**
¾ cup **all-purpose flour**, sifted

1 **egg**, beaten
Zest of 1 **lime**
⅓ cup **sugar**

FOR THE DULCE DE LECHE

Place the condensed milk into a saucepot and cover it with water.

Bring it to a boil then turn the heat to a simmer and cook for 6–8 hours. The longer you cook it the darker the caramel will be.

Add hot water to the pot as needed to keep the can completely submerged.

After 6–8 hours, turn off the heat. Let the can cool before removing it from the water and place in the refrigerator overnight.

The next day, use a stand mixer with the whisk attachment to whip the caramel for about a minute. Adding air to the dulce de leche will make it soft and dippable for the churros.

FOR THE CHURROS

Preheat a deep fryer filled with canola oil to 350°F.

In a small saucepot, combine the water, salt, and butter and bring it to a boil on high heat.

Turn off the heat and add the flour, mixing with a wooden spoon until the dough comes together.

Add the dough to a stand mixer with the whisk attachment and allow it to cool for about 5 minutes.

Turn the mixer on medium speed and add the beaten egg. Mix the dough until it comes together again, about 2–3 minutes.

Put the dough into a piping bag with a large star tip and let the dough cool to room temperature.

In a large bowl mix the lime zest and sugar and set it aside.

Add a touch of oil to a pair of kitchen scissors. Pipe the dough into the hot fryer, carefully cutting off 3-inch pieces.

Cook the churros for about 4 minutes. Use tongs to turn them for even browning.

Remove the churros, toss them with the lime sugar, and serve with the whipped dulce de leche.

CHEF NOTES

You can also pipe the dough out onto a baking tray lined with parchment paper and freeze it for 5–10 minutes. Then the churros can be dropped by hand into the fryer.

Strawberry and Cream Terrarium

A terrarium is a beautiful arrangement of soils, rocks, and plants, usually presented in a glass container, vase, or aquarium. For this recipe, I have recreated the beauty of a terrarium as a delicious strawberry and cream dessert. It's composed of layers of light, fluffy vanilla and strawberry-infused mousse with macerated red berries, fresh herbs, edible soil, and chocolate twigs.

Impress your guests at your next dinner party, or try this dessert layered with pieces of shortcake presented in a trifle dish for a family-style treat.

Yield: Serves 6
Preparation time: 2–3 hours
Cook time: 1 hour

Specialty equipment
Thermometer
Piping bag + fine tip
Fine mesh strainer
Stand mixer

Edible Soil
¾ cup **gluten-free panko crumbs**
3 tsp **cocoa powder**
½ tsp **canola oil**
1 tsp **sugar**
¼ tsp **activated charcoal**

Chocolate Sticks
1 lb **65% chocolate**

Strawberry Purée
1½ lb **frozen strawberries**

Strawberry Mousse
1½ cups **heavy cream**
7 oz **strawberry purée**
⅔ cup **sugar**
2 sheets **gelatin** (3 g)

Vanilla Mousse
1⅓ cup **heavy cream**, divided
2 tbsp **sugar**
1 **Madagascar vanilla bean**
2 sheets **gelatin** (3 g)

Finishing the Plate
7 oz **fresh strawberries**
1 tsp **sugar**
Strawberry purée
Fresh mint and **basil** for garnish

FOR THE EDIBLE SOIL

Preheat oven to 350°F.

Lightly toast the panko crumbs in the oven for 3–5 minutes, until golden brown. I prefer to use gluten-free crumbs for this recipe because of the texture. They are made with rice flour and have a larger-sized grain than regular panko crumbs. Puffed rice could be used as a substitute.

Put the panko into a mixing bowl with the rest of the ingredients and combine. The crumbs should resemble potting soil.

FOR THE CHOCOLATE STICKS

Pour about 2 inches of water into a saucepot and turn it on medium heat.

Chop the chocolate up fine and add ⅔ of it to a mixing bowl that fits over the top of the pot.

Melt the chocolate, stirring occasionally so it will melt evenly.

Using a thermometer, heat the chocolate to 131°F.

Remove the chocolate from the pot and add the other ⅓ of chocolate to the bowl. Stir the chocolate as it melts and cool the temperature to 82.4°F.

When the chocolate reaches 82.4°F, put it back over the pot and heat it to 89.6°F.

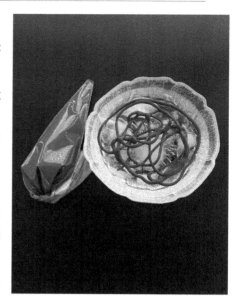

Remove the chocolate from the heat. It is now tempered, giving it a nice shine and snappy texture when cooled.

Add the tempered chocolate to a piping bag with a fine tip.

Set up a bowl with ice water.

Pipe the chocolate into the bowl in irregular shapes. This will set the chocolate almost immediately. Remove the chocolate and place it on a paper towel to dry.

You may not need all the chocolate for this recipe. It can be saved and tempered again.

FOR THE STRAWBERRY PURÉE

Put the strawberries into a saucepot and cook them over low heat for about 30 minutes. Stir occasionally to prevent burning.

Pour the cooked berries into a blender and purée until smooth.

Press through a fine mesh strainer and set aside to cool.

FOR THE STRAWBERRY MOUSSE

Whip the heavy cream using a stand mixer with the whisk attachment to stiff peaks and set it aside.

In a small bowl, soak the gelatin sheets in cold water.

Set up a large mixing bowl with ice and water in it.

Place the strawberry purée and sugar in a saucepot and bring to a boil. Stir to prevent burning. Once it comes to a boil, turn off the heat.

Remove the gelatin sheets from the water, squeeze out any excess, and whisk into the strawberry mix to melt.

Pour the hot mixture into a large mixing bowl and place over the ice bath to cool. Continuously stir the mix with a spatula, scraping down the sides of the bowl to prevent the gelatin from setting.

When it starts to become thick and cool to the touch, remove the bowl from the ice bath and fold in the whipped cream. Make sure the strawberry mix is cold; if it is still warm, the whipped cream will melt.

Divide the mix over six bowls and set it aside in the fridge while you prepare the vanilla mousse layer.

FOR THE VANILLA MOUSSE

Whip ⅔ cup of heavy cream to stiff peaks and set it aside.

In a small bowl, soak the gelatin sheets in cold water.

Set up a mixing bowl with ice and water.

Pour the other ⅔ cup of heavy cream and sugar into a saucepot.

Split the vanilla bean pod in half lengthwise and scrape the seeds from each side of the pod. Add the seeds and the empty vanilla bean pod to the cream and bring it to a boil on high heat. Stir continuously to prevent burning.

Once the cream boils, turn off the heat and remove the vanilla bean pod. Discard.

Squeeze the excess water from the gelatin sheets and whisk them into the hot cream to melt.

Pour the cream into a mixing bowl and place it over the ice bath. Mix it continuously with a spatula until it is cold to the touch but not yet starting to set.

Remove the bowl from the ice bath and fold in the whipped cream.

Pour the mix on top of the strawberry layer and let the mousse set for 1 hour in the refrigerator.

FINISHING THE PLATE

Slice the fresh strawberries and place them in a bowl with the sugar. Let this sit until the strawberries become soft and syrupy.

Garnish the top of the mousse with the rest of the strawberry purée, edible soil, macerated strawberries, fresh mint, basil leaves and chocolate sticks.

CHEF NOTES

Activated charcoal gives the edible soil a rich, dark brown colour creating the illusion of real soil.

Pumpkin Sticky Toffee Pudding

Pumpkin sticky toffee pudding was a signature dessert on the fall menu at our restaurant, Black Pig. In this recipe, pumpkin purée is used as a substitute for the dates in traditional sticky toffee pudding. The salted molasses sauce adds bittersweetness that complements the spiciness of the candied ginger and the tartness from the crème fraîche, creating the perfect balance of flavours.

Yield: 6 cakes; 3 cups of sauce
Preparation time: 12–16 hours + overnight
Cook time: 1 hour

Specialty equipment
Stand mixer
Ramakins
Cooling rack

Crème Fraîche

2 cups **heavy cream**
¾ cup **buttermilk**
Juice from half a **lemon**

Pumpkin Cake

3 oz **butter**
¾ cup **brown sugar**
¼ cup **fancy molasses**
1¼ tbsp **honey**
½ tsp **vanilla**
2 **eggs**
1¼ cup **all-purpose flour**
¾ cup **pumpkin purée**
½ cup **water**
1 tsp **baking soda**

Finishing the Plate

4 oz **butter**
2 cups **heavy cream**
1 cup **brown sugar**
¼ cup **fancy molasses**
1 tsp **salt**
¼ cup **candied ginger**, chopped

FOR THE CRÈME FRAÎCHE

Combine the ingredients in a mixing bowl and stir.

Wrap the bowl and place it in a warm area in the kitchen for 12 hours.

The mixture will become thick like yogurt. If it looks runny still, leave it to sit longer.

Line a strainer with cheesecloth set over a bowl. Pour the crème fraîche into the strainer and allow it to drain in the refrigerator overnight.

FOR THE PUMPKIN CAKE

Preheat oven to 350°F.

Set up a stand mixer with the paddle attachment.

Cream together the butter, brown sugar, honey, and molasses. Add the vanilla and mix.

Next, add the eggs, one at a time. Stop the mixer and scrape down the sides of the bowl to ensure all the ingredients are evenly incorporated.

Sift the flour and add it slowly to the mixer on low speed. Turn off the mixer.

In a small pot on high heat, whisk the pumpkin purée and water together and cook until it boils. Stir this continuously. Be careful when it boils; it will pop a bit as it is quite thick.

Remove the pumpkin from the heat.

Add the baking soda. Only mix once or twice to stir in the soda; don't overmix.

Turn the mixer on low speed and gradually add the pumpkin purée by the spoonful until everything is incorporated.

Coat the inside of 6 ramekins with non-stick spray. Place inside a large ovenproof dish.

Fill each ramekins three-quarters full of cake mix.

Pour about 2 inches of water into the bottom of the baking dish. Cover with foil and bake the cakes in the oven for 25 minutes or until a toothpick inserted comes out clean.

Remove the cakes from the ramekins onto a cooling rack.

FINISHING THE PLATE

Whisk everything, except the ginger, together in a small pot and bring it to a boil on high heat.

Turn off the heat.

Add a warm pumpkin cake to the center of a plate. Pour sauce over the pumpkin cake.

Top with a scoop of crème fraîche and a sprinkle of chopped candied ginger.

CHEF NOTES

This cake can also be baked in a square brownie pan and cut into portions.

Notes

Vermouth

I remember the first time I tried vermouth as a cocktail on its own. We were in Spain at a tapas restaurant, and when we sat down were asked if we would like the welcome cocktail. It was vermouth infused with orange peel—simple and delicious, the perfect pairing for the bites that followed.

Vermouth was historically used for medicinal purposes; it is a fortified wine infused with various botanicals. Today, it is served as an aperitif or an ingredient in other cocktails. In this recipe, I have added chinotto, a bittersweet carbonated soft drink made from the fruit of the myrtle-leaved orange tree. Serve this cocktail at the start or the end of a meal.

Yield: 1 cocktail
Preparation time: 5 minutes

2 oz **red (sweet) vermouth**
Orange peel
Chinotto

FOR THE VERMOUTH

Add ice to an 8-oz rocks glass and pour the vermouth overtop.

Using a channel knife, cut a few strips of zest from the orange. Do this directly over the glass to catch the fragrant orange oils that are released when the zest is cut. A vegetable peeler will also work if you do not have a channel knife.

Top the beverage with chinotto. Stir gently and serve.

CHEF NOTES

I prefer to make this cocktail with a large ice cube. With less surface area, they melt slower than many small cubes, which tend to water down the cocktail.

Yuzu Jalapeño Lemonade

This refreshing variation on lemonade is easy to make, has a hint of spice, and uses yuzu instead of lemon. Yuzu is a tart fragrant citrus fruit mainly cultivated in east Asia. It is typically not found fresh in North America, but instead sold as juice or condiment.

Yuzu gives this popular summertime beverage a unique floral aroma when combined with the spice of the fresh jalapeño and the sweetness of the simple syrup.

Yield: **2 yuzu lemonades**
Preparation time: **20 minutes**

Specialty equipment
Muddler

Simple Syrup
½ cup **sugar**
½ cup w**ater**

Yuzu Lemonade
½ **jalapeño**
2 tbsp **simple syrup**
¼ cup **yuzu juice**
Soda water

Salt Sugar Rim
¼ cup **sugar**
2 tbsp **coarse salt**

FOR THE SIMPLE SYRUP

Mix the sugar and water in a saucepot.

Bring it to a boil on high heat and reduce it by half.

Turn off the heat and let the syrup cool.

FOR THE RIM

In a small bowl mix the sugar and salt.

CHEF NOTES

This yuzu lemonade would be great with an ounce of your favourite gin or vodka added to it for a delicious cocktail.

FOR THE YUZU LEMONADE

Chop the half jalapeño, keeping its seeds if you prefer a spicy version or removing them for a milder hint of spice. Place into a cocktail-mixing pitcher.

Add the simple syrup and a cube of ice; smash it up well using a muddler.

Stir in the yuzu juice.

Use a wedge of lemon to wet the rims of two glasses and dip them into the salt and sugar mix.

Add ice and strain the yuzu mix into each glass. Top it with soda water and fresh slices of jalapeno.

Sangria

Sangria is a punch traditionally made with wine and fresh chopped fruit; sometimes fruit juices or spirits are added. One of the most popular beverages in Spain, sangria is served at restaurants, bars, and during festivities in both Spain and Portugal.

In this recipe, I'll share two of my favourite versions of this delicious beverage. One is made with red wine, grape juice, and orange; the other is made with white wine, peaches, and fresh lime. Serve this refreshing low-alcohol drink topped with soda water. It will be a hit at your next BBQ or outdoor event.

Yield: Serves 4
Preparation time: 25 minutes

Red Sangria
1 bottle of **red wine, grenache**
1 cup **grape juice**
1 tbsp Simple Syrup (recipe on page 137)
1 cup **grapes**
1 cup **blackberries**
1 **orange**, juiced
1 **orange**, sliced

White Sangria
1 bottle of **sweet white wine**, such as Riesling
½ cup **raspberries**
1 **peach**, sliced
1 **lime**, sliced
1 tbsp Simple Syrup (recipe on page 137)
1 cup **peach juice**

MIXING THE SANGRIA

Freeze the berries and grapes before making the sangria. I like to have all the ingredients as cold as possible so that the sangria doesn't get watered down by ice.

Combine everything in a pitcher, for the type of sangria you choose to make.

Add some ice to a wine glass and fill it with sangria. Garnish the edge of the glass with fresh fruit.

CHEF NOTES

Try adding spirits to your sangria, such as brandy or cointreau. You may also want to substitute Cava for white wine to make a refreshing sparkling sangria.

Chanterelle Mushroom-Infused Vodka Caesar

The Caesar is Canada's national cocktail. It was invented here in Calgary in 1969 and the original recipe contained vodka, tomato juice, clam nectar, Worcestershire, and celery salt.

For this version of the classic cocktail, maple bacon, lemon, and Clamato juice are paired with the earthiness of the chanterelle mushroom-infused vodka.

Chanterelle mushrooms are orange, yellow, or white funnel-shaped mushrooms with a smooth rounded cap. Choose your mushrooms during the peak of the season to capture the light apricot aroma and almost peppery flavour that will saturate the vodka.

Yield: **26-oz bottle**
Preparation time: **25 minutes + 1 week**
Infusion time: **1 week**

Chanterelle Mushroom-Infused Vodka
1 x 26-oz bottle of **good-quality vodka**
⅓ lb **fresh chanterelle mushrooms**

Caesar
Thick sliced Maple Bacon (recipe on page 19)
Fresh **lemon**
Celery salt
2 oz **chanterelle mushroom vodka**
1 tsp Hot Sauce (recipe on page 13)

Splash of **Worcestershire sauce**
Clamato juice
Celery leaves (garnish) ⅓ lb fresh
Chanterelle mushrooms

FOR THE VODKA

Brush any dirt off the chanterelle mushrooms. Place them into a sealable container and pour the vodka over top. Let the mixture sit for at least 1 week. The longer it sits the more intense the chanterelle mushroom flavour becomes.

FOR THE CAESAR

Preheat oven to 375°F.

Cut thick slices of the maple bacon and place them on a tray lined with parchment paper. Cook the bacon slices in the oven until they start to get crispy, 5–10 minutes.

Remove the bacon from the oven, place it on a paper towel and set it aside while you make the Caesar.

Place the celery salt in a small bowl.

Cut a lemon wedge and rub it along the rim of a 16-oz glass, then coat it with the celery salt.

Fill the glass with ice. Add the vodka, hot sauce, Worcestershire sauce, and top with Clamato juice. Garnish the drink with the crispy maple bacon, lemon wedge, and celery leaves.

CHEF NOTES

The mushroom-infused vodka can be used in other cocktails or shaken over ice for a martini with olives.

Notes

CPSIA information can be obtained
at www.ICGtesting.com
Printed in the USA
BVHW060059011222
653087BV00001B/2